Contents

Introduction

The contents of this book are based upon the National Science Education Standards for Grade 4. These standards include (A) Unifying Concepts and Processes, (B) Science as Inquiry, (C) Physical Science, (D) Life Science, (E) Earth and Space Science, (F) Science and Technology, (G) Science in Personal and Social Perspectives, and (H) History and Nature of Science.

This book will help teachers, students, parents, and tutors. Teachers can use this book either to introduce or review a topic in their science classroom. Students will find the book useful in reviewing the major concepts in science. Parents can use this book to help their children with topics that may be posing a problem in the classroom. Tutors can use this book as a basis for their lessons and for assigning questions and activities.

This book includes nine lessons that focus on the nine major concepts presented in the content standards: Physical Science, Life Science, and Earth and Space Science. The lessons also cover the sixteen major concepts presented in the other standards. A table on page 4 provides a correlation between the contents of each lesson and the National Science Education Standards.

Before beginning the book, the reader can check his or her knowledge of the content by completing the *Assessment*. The *Assessment* consists of questions that deal with the content standards. This will allow the reader to determine how much he or she knows about a particular concept before beginning to read about it. The *Assessment* may also serve as a way of leading the reader to a specific lesson that may be of special interest.

Each lesson follows the same sequence in presenting the material. A list of *Key Terms* is always provided at the beginning of each lesson. This list includes all the bold-faced terms and their definitions presented in the same order that they are introduced in the lesson. The reader can develop a sense of the lesson content by glancing through the *Key Terms*. Each lesson then provides background information about the concept. This information is divided into several sections. Each section is written so that the reader is not overwhelmed with details. Rather, the reader is guided through the concept in a logical sequence. Each lesson then moves on to a *Review*. This section consists of several multiple-choice and short-answer questions. The multiple-choice questions check if the reader has retained information that was covered in the lesson. The short-

answer questions check if the reader can use information from the lesson to provide the answers.

Each lesson then moves on to a series of activities. These activities are designed to check the reader's understanding of the information. Some activities extend the lesson by presenting additional information. The activities are varied so as not to be boring. For example, reading passages about interesting and unusual findings are included. Questions to check reading comprehension are then asked. As a change of pace, some activities are meant to engage the reader in a "fun-type" exercise. These activities include crosswords, word searches, jumbled letters, and cryptograms.

The last activity in each lesson is an experiment. Each experiment has been designed so that the required items are easy to locate and can usually be found in most households. Care has been taken to avoid the use of any dangerous materials or chemicals. However, an adult should always be present when a student is conducting an experiment. In some cases, the experimental procedure reminds students that adult supervision is required. Before beginning any experiment, an adult should review the list of materials and the procedure. In this way, the adult will be aware of any situations that may need special attention. The adult should review the safety issues before the experiment is begun. The adult may want to check a laboratory manual for specific safety precautions that should be followed when doing an experiment, such as wearing safety goggles and never touching or tasting chemicals.

The book then follows with a *Science Fair Projects* section. Information is presented on how to conduct and present a science fair project. In some cases, the experiment at the end of a lesson can serve as the basis for a science fair project. Additional suggestions are also provided with advice on how to choose an award-winning science fair project.

A *Glossary* is next. This section lists all the boldfaced terms in alphabetical order and indicates the page on which the term is used. The book concludes with an *Answer Key*, which gives the answers to all the activity questions, including the experiment.

This book has been designed and written so that teachers, students, parents, and tutors will find it easy to use and follow. Most importantly, students will benefit from this book by achieving at a higher level in class and on standardized tests.

National Science Education Standards

Standard A: UNIFYING CONCEPTS AND PROCESSES

A1 Systems, order, and organization
A2 Evidence, models, and explanation
A3 Change, constancy, and measurement
A4 Evolution and equilibrium
A5 Form and function

Standard B: SCIENCE AS INQUIRY

B1 Abilities necessary to do scientific inquiry
B2 Understanding about scientific inquiry

Standard C: PHYSICAL SCIENCE

C1 Properties of objects and materials
C2 Position and motion of objects
C3 Light, heat, electricity, and magnetism

Standard D: LIFE SCIENCE

D1 Characteristics of organisms
D2 Life cycles of organisms
D3 Organisms and environments

Standard E: EARTH AND SPACE SCIENCE

E1 Properties of earth materials
E2 Objects in the sky
E3 Changes in earth and sky

Standard F: SCIENCE AND TECHNOLOGY

F1 Abilities to distinguish between natural objects and objects made by humans
F2 Abilities of technological design
F3 Understanding about science and technology

Standard G: SCIENCE IN PERSONAL AND SOCIAL PERSPECTIVES

G1 Personal health
G2 Characteristics and changes in populations
G3 Types of resources
G4 Changes in environments
G5 Science and technology in local challenges

Standard H: HISTORY AND NATURE OF SCIENCE

H1 Science as a human endeavor

Correlation to National Science Education Standards

Unit 1: Physical Science
Lesson 1: Properties of Objects and Materials
Background Information A3, C1, B1
Review A5, C1
Properties of Matter. C1
Solids, Liquids, and Gases. C1
States of Matter C1
Titanic C1, F2, G5
Experiment: Mass, Volume, and Density . . B2, C1

Lesson 2: Position and Motion of Objects
Background Information A3, C2
Review C2
Position C2
Position and Motion C2
Breaking the Sound Barrier. C2, F3, H1
Experiment: Investigating Motion. . . B1, A3, C2

Lesson 3: Light, Heat, Electricity, and Magnetism
Background Information A1, C3
Review. C3, F1
Describing Forms of Energy C3
Heat Transfer C3
Electric Circuits. C3
Comparing Forms of Energy. C3
Experiment: Investigating Reflection . B1, C3, F2

Unit 2: Life Science
Lesson 4: Characteristics of Organisms
Background Information D1, F1
Review D1
Types of Cells. D1
Prefixes D1
Describing Living Things D1
Discovering Cells. D1, H1
Experiment: Getting Too Close. B1, D1, G2

Lesson 5: Life Cycles of Organisms
Background Information A3, D2
Review D2
Growing Up D2
Describing Change. D2
Insect Life Cycles D2
The Monarch Butterfly D2, G4
Experiment: The Parts of a Flower. . . A2, B2, D2

Lesson 6: Organisms and Environments
Background Information A1, D3, G2
Review D3
A Frozen Food Chain D3
Making Predictions D3
Describing Organisms. D3
Biomes of the World. A1, D3
Experiment: Insect Habitats B2, D3, G4

Unit 3: Earth and Space Science
Lesson 7: Properties of Earth Materials
Background Information A2, E1, G3
Review E1
Earth's Materials E1
Properties of Minerals and Rocks E1
The Grand Canyon A4, E1
Experiment: Investigating
Weathering A3, B1, E1

Lesson 8: Objects in the Sky
Background Information A1, E2
Review E2
Shooting Stars E2
Describing Objects in the Sky E2
Supernovas. A2, E2
Experiment: Investigating Star Brightness. B2, E2

Lesson 9: Changes in Earth and Sky
Background Information A3, E3
Review E3
Naming Constellations E3
Constellation Stories E3, H1
Experiment: Investigating Moon Phases. . A2, E3

Assessment

Darken the circle by the best answer.

Lesson 1

1. In which state can matter be compressed into a smaller container?

   (A) liquid   (C) gas

   (B) solid   (D) chemical

2. What is the volume of a box that measures 2 cm by 3 cm by 10 cm?

   (A) 15 cm^3 (C) 32 cm^3

   (B) 16 cm^3 (D) 60 cm^3

Lesson 2

3. A person sitting on a bus driving down the street is NOT moving relative to

   (A) a bird flying above it.

   (B) the bus driver.

   (C) the street.

   (D) a tree.

4. An object's speed is the distance it travels divided by

   (A) the length of the object.

   (B) the volume of the object.

   (C) the mass of the object.

   (D) the time it took to travel that distance.

Lesson 3

5. What happens when light is reflected from an object?

   (A) It bounces back from the object.

   (B) It is bent by the object.

   (C) It is absorbed by the object.

   (D) It passes straight through the object.

6. What happens when two like magnetic poles are brought together?

   (A) They pull together.

   (B) They push apart.

   (C) Both magnets lose their magnetism.

   (D) The magnets become one.

Lesson 4

7. What gas do animals give off that is used by plants during photosynthesis?

   (A) nitrogen   (C) oxygen

   (B) air   (D) carbon dioxide

8. What is one reason that lizards lie on rocks in the sun?

   (A) to cool off

   (B) to get warm

   (C) to look for food

   (D) to get water

Lesson 5

9. What is metamorphosis?

   (A) a tool scientists use to study organisms

   (B) a method through which organisms stay warm

   (C) a process through which organisms grow and change

   (D) a process through which animals move to warm places in winter

10. What is the first stage for plants that make flowers?

    (A) seed   (C) cone

    (B) spore   (D) tadpole

Assessment, page 2

Lesson 6

11. Which of these is a species?

(A) all of the plants and animals in a zoo

(B) all of the animals in a zoo

(C) all of the mammals in a zoo

(D) all of the Bengal tigers in a zoo

12. Which of these is a producer in an ecosystem?

(A) mouse   (C) grass

(B) hawk   (D) grasshopper

Lesson 7

13. What does the luster of a mineral describe?

(A) what color it is

(B) how shiny it is

(C) how hard it is

(D) how it breaks

14. Which type of rock is formed from a volcanic eruption?

(A) metamorphic   (C) igneous

(B) sedimentary   (D) lunar

Lesson 8

15. What is a star?

(A) a ball of melting ice

(B) a spinning piece of dust

(C) a rock that is moving very fast

(D) a glowing ball of gas

16. The path a planet takes around the sun is called its

(A) orbit.   (C) axis.

(B) moon.   (D) core.

Lesson 9

17. Which movement causes day and night?

(A) Earth's revolution

(B) Earth's rotation

(C) the moon's revolution

(D) the sun's rotation

18. How is Earth positioned on the first day of fall in the Northern Hemisphere?

(A) The Northern Hemisphere points toward the sun.

(B) The Northern Hemisphere points away from the sun.

(C) Neither hemisphere points toward or away from the sun.

(D) Both hemispheres point toward the sun.

Lesson 1 Properties of Objects and Materials

Look around you. What do you see? Maybe you see books, desks, windows, walls, and even people. All of the objects and materials you can name are examples of **matter**. Matter is made up of smaller parts called particles. Particles of matter are so small that scientists must use special types of microscopes to see them. These particles are constantly moving.

States of Matter

The arrangement of the particles of matter determines the state of matter. There are three common states of matter: solid, liquid, or gas.

Solids This book, the chair you are sitting in, and your desk are examples of matter in the solid state. A **solid** has a definite shape. This means that the shape of this book will not change whether you move it from your desk to your backpack to your kitchen table. In addition, it will always take up the same amount of space. If you try to squeeze it into a small box, it simply won't fit. You cannot make it smaller.

Key Terms

matter—any material or object that has mass and takes up space

solid—the state of matter that has a definite shape and takes up a definite amount of space

liquid—the state of matter that takes up a definite amount of space but takes the shape of its container

gas—the state of matter that has no definite shape and takes up no definite amount of space

mass—the amount of matter in an object

volume—the amount of space an object or material takes up

density—the mass of an object divided by its volume

physical property—a characteristic of matter that can be observed without changing the nature of the matter

chemical property—a characteristic of matter that can be observed only by changing the nature of the matter

A solid keeps its shape and size because its particles are packed closely together. Each particle is tightly fixed to its position. Although the particles can move back and forth, they stay in place.

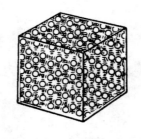

Liquids What did you drink with breakfast today? Perhaps you drank water, juice, or milk. These drinks are examples of matter in the **liquid** state. Like a solid, the amount of space a liquid takes up does not change. This means that if you pour a cup of juice into a large bowl, the amount of juice does not increase or decrease. Unlike a solid, however, the shape of a liquid can change. A liquid will take the shape of its container.

In a liquid, the particles are packed together, but they are free to slide past one another. Although individual particles can move around, all of the particles in a liquid stay close together. The movement of liquid particles is what makes it possible to pour a liquid. It is also what makes a liquid take the shape of its container.

Gases The air around you and the helium in a balloon are examples of gases. A **gas** is matter that does not have a definite shape and does not take up a definite amount of space.

The particles in a gas are constantly moving at high speeds in all directions. They hit each other and the walls of their container. If the particles do not hit anything, they will keep moving. A gas will therefore expand, or spread apart, to fill its container. A gas can also be squeezed, or compressed, into a smaller container.

Mass

No matter what the state, all samples of matter can be described by their mass. **Mass** is the amount of matter something contains. A marble has more mass than an identical ball of foam. A golf ball, for example, has more mass than a table tennis ball.

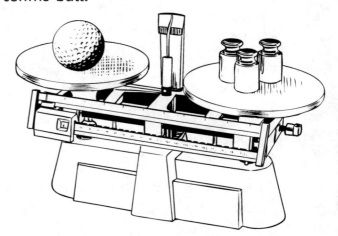

You can measure the mass of an object using a tool called a balance. To use a balance, place the object you are measuring on one pan. Place objects with

Lesson 1, Properties of Objects and Materials
Science 4, SV 9781419034329

known masses on the other pan until the two pans are balanced. If you add up the masses of the known objects, you will find the mass of the object you are measuring. Small masses are measured in units called grams (g). Larger masses can be measured in kilograms (kg). There are 1,000 grams in 1 kilogram.

Volume

Even though they have different masses, a golf ball has something in common with a table tennis ball. They take up about the same amount of space. The amount of space that an object takes up is called its **volume**. How you measure volume depends on the type of matter you are measuring.

Volume of Liquids You may have measured the volume of a liquid if you have filled a measuring cup with milk for a recipe. To find the volume of a liquid, pour the liquid into a container marked with units of measurement. Scientists use tools such as beakers and graduated cylinders to measure volume. The basic unit of volume is the liter (L). Smaller volumes can be measured in milliliters (mL). There are 1,000 milliliters in 1 liter.

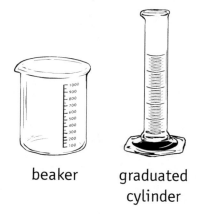

beaker   graduated cylinder

Volume of Regular Solids A brick and a shoe box are examples of regular solids. To find the volume of a regular solid, you can use a ruler to measure the length, width, and height. Then multiply the measurements together.

Volume = length $\times$ width $\times$ height
If each measurement is made in centimeters, the unit of volume will be cubic centimeters (cm^3). A cubic centimeter is the space taken up by a cube that measures 1 centimeter on each side.

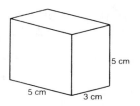

5 cm
5 cm   3 cm

You can find the volume of the cube above by multiplying.

$$V = 5 \text{ cm} \times 3 \text{ cm} \times 5 \text{ cm}$$
$$V = 75 \text{ cm}^3$$

Volume of Odd-Shaped Solids Not all solids have regular shapes. Suppose you want to find the volume of an odd-shaped stone. You can place the stone into a container of water. When the stone sinks in the water, it causes the level of the water to rise. The change in the water level is the volume of the stone.

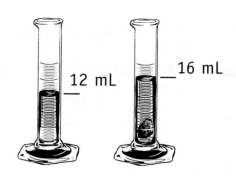

12 mL   16 mL

Lesson 1, Properties of Objects and Materials
Science 4, SV 9781419034329

Density

You know that a golf ball and a table tennis ball have a different mass but about the same volume. In other words, the golf ball has more mass in the same amount of volume. The amount of mass compared to volume is known as **density**. The density of the golf ball is greater than the density of the table tennis ball. You can find the density of an object by dividing its mass by its volume.

Density can be used to explain why some objects float and others sink. An object will float if it is placed into a substance with a greater density. For example, a tennis ball will float in water because the density of the ball is less than the density of water. The density of a golf ball is greater than the density of water. What do you think will happen to a golf ball hit into a pool of water? You are correct if you predicted that the golf ball will sink.

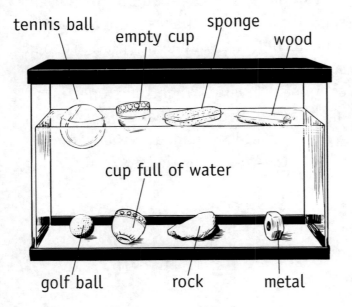

tennis ball
empty cup
sponge
wood

cup full of water

golf ball   rock   metal

Physical and Chemical Properties

So far you have been learning about physical properties of matter. A **physical property** is one that you can describe without changing the sample. For example, you can look at a wall and see that it is blue. You can measure the mass or volume of a skateboard. You can see that water is in the liquid state. You can feel the texture of a turtle's shell. Color, mass, volume, state, and texture are just a few of the many physical properties of matter.

Some properties of matter are chemical properties. A **chemical property** is one that you can identify only as the matter is changing. The ability to burn is an example of a chemical property. When you look at the tip of a match, you cannot see this property. However, when the match is struck against a hard surface, it begins to burn. When it is finished burning, the matter has changed.

If you ever leave a metal object, such as your bicycle, out in the rain, you might observe another chemical property—the ability to rust. Rusting happens more slowly than burning does, but it also involves a change in matter.

Lesson 1

Review

Darken the circle by the best answer.

1. Matter in the liquid state has a definite
- (A) shape.
- (B) volume.
- (C) color.
- (D) container.

2. Which is an object's mass?
- (A) its color
- (B) its shape
- (C) how much matter it has
- (D) how much space it takes up

3. Which sentence best describes a gas?
- (A) The particles are held in fixed positions.
- (B) The particles slide past each other.
- (C) The particles are connected in long chains.
- (D) The particles move freely in all directions.

4. Which unit of measurement can you use to describe volume?
- (A) milliliter (mL)
- (B) gram (g)
- (C) meter (m)
- (D) kilogram (kg)

5. The density of an object is equal to its mass divided by its
- (A) length.
- (B) volume.
- (C) height.
- (D) particles.

6. Which of these is a chemical property of matter?
- (A) mass
- (B) ability to burn
- (C) volume
- (D) density

7. How does the arrangement of particles determine the properties of solids, liquids, and gases?

_____

_____

_____

8. How is a chemical property different from a physical property? Give examples of each.

_____

_____

_____

Lesson 1   Properties of Matter

Fill in the puzzle with the terms described by each clue. Choose from the word box below.

chemical	gas	liquid	matter	solid
color	gram	liter	meter	volume
density	length	mass	physical	

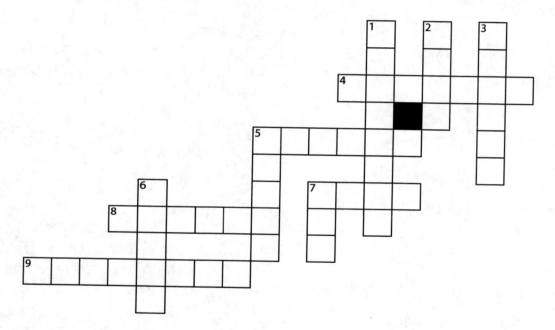

Across

4. The mass of an object divided by its volume

5. A sample of matter that has a definite volume but not a definite shape

7. A unit of mass

8. The amount of space an object takes up

9. A type of property that can be observed without changing the sample of matter

Down

1. A type of property that describes a change in matter

2. The amount of matter in an object

3. Anything that has mass and takes up space

5. A unit of volume

6. An object made up of particles that are held tightly in place

7. The state of matter made up of particles that can expand to fill their container

Lesson 1   Solids, Liquids, and Gases

Write a key term to complete each sentence. Choose from the words below.

chemical	liquid	physical
density	mass	solid
gas	matter	volume

1. The particles in a _____ have greater movement than the particles in a liquid.

2. The _____ of a bird is the amount of matter it contains.

3. A pitcher can hold a greater _____ of juice than a cup can.

4. The size of a box is one of its _____ properties.

5. Trees, rocks, and lemonade are examples of _____ because they all have mass and volume.

6. When you say that paper can burn, you are describing a _____ property of paper.

7. To find the _____ of an object, divide its mass by its volume.

8. In a _____, the particles of matter are held closely together.

9. A _____ is a type of matter that has a definite volume but not a definite shape.

Lesson 1

States of Matter

Look at the diagrams shown. Label each one as a solid, a liquid, or a gas.
Beside each one, list at least two examples of each.

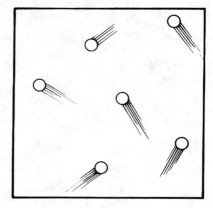

_____

_____

_____

_____

_____

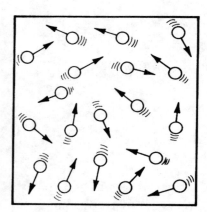

_____

_____

_____

_____

_____

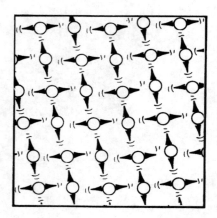

_____

_____

_____

_____

_____

Lesson 1, States of Matter
Science 4, SV 9781419034329

Lesson 1

Titanic

Read the following passage. Then answer the questions that follow the passage.

On April 10, 1912, a ship known as the *Titanic* set sail on its very first trip. It was traveling from England to New York City. Like other ships, the density of the materials used to build the *Titanic* was greater than the density of water. To make the ship float, air was locked into parts of the ship. The density of air is much lower than the density of water, so the air helps the ship to float.

The *Titanic* was built with several air-filled sections along the bottom. The builders predicted that the ship would still float even if some of these sections became filled with water. They called the ship unsinkable.

Four days into the trip, the *Titanic* struck an iceberg. An iceberg is a huge piece of ice floating in open water. The density of an iceberg is just a little less than the density of sea water. This causes the iceberg to float, but most of an iceberg stays under water. Only a little part of it rises above the water's surface. This makes it hard for people on ships to figure out the true shape and size of an entire iceberg.

The iceberg ripped holes in some of the air-filled sections at the bottom of the ship. When too many of the sections became filled with water, the ship could no longer float. Just hours later, the *Titanic* sank to the bottom of the ocean.

Titanic (cont'd.)

1. What is the reason for locking air in parts of a ship?

   (A) to make the air larger

   (B) so passengers can have air to breathe

   (C) to lower the density of the ship

   (D) to make the ship move faster

2. The density of ice is

   (A) much lower than the density of sea water.

   (B) a little lower than the density of sea water.

   (C) a little greater than the density of sea water.

   (D) much greater than the density of sea water.

3. Why is it hard for ship captains to see all of an iceberg?

   (A) Most of an iceberg's volume is under water.

   (B) An iceberg is the same color as the sky.

   (C) Icebergs sink to the bottom of the ocean.

   (D) Icebergs move along with ships.

4. What caused the *Titanic* to sink?

   (A) The builders added too much metal to it.

   (B) Too many people were traveling on the ship.

   (C) The water became too cold for the ship to move.

   (D) Its density became greater than the density of ocean water.

Lesson 1   Experiment: Mass, Volume, and Density

In this lesson you learned that an object can be described by its mass, volume, and density. Can objects have the same volume but different masses? How do changes in mass affect density? In this experiment, you will find the answers to these questions.

What You Will Need

small plastic drinking bottle (or similar item such as a film canister or baby bottle)
several quarters or other coins
plastic or metal bowl
water
balance or kitchen scale

Procedure

1. Place one quarter in the bottle and screw the lid on.

2. Use the balance to find the mass of the bottle and coin. Record the mass in the data table.

3. Fill the bowl about three-fourths full with water.

4. Gently place the bottle in the water. Observe whether it floats or sinks. Record your observation in the data table.

5. Remove the lid from the bottle. Add two quarters and replace the lid. Again use the balance to find the mass of the bottle. Record the mass in the data table.

6. Again place the bottle in the water to determine whether it floats or sinks. Record your observation in the data table.

7. Repeat steps 5–7, adding two more quarters each time until the bottle sinks.

Experiment: Mass, Volume, and Density (cont'd.)

Number of quarters	Mass	Float or Sink
1 ✓	25g	float
3		
5		

Analysis

1. Did the volume of the bottle change throughout the experiment? Explain.

_____

_____

_____

2. Did the mass of the bottle change throughout the experiment? Explain.

_____

_____

_____

Conclusion

Based on your observations, what can you conclude about the density of the bottle throughout the experiment? Explain your answer.

_____

_____

_____

Lesson 2 Position and Motion of Objects

What kinds of examples come to mind when you think about objects that are moving? Perhaps you imagine a horse running across a field. Maybe you think of a baseball soaring through the air. You might even picture yourself running, swimming, or riding on a skateboard. Do you consider yourself sitting at your desk or sleeping in bed? You might be surprised to find out that you are moving even when you are doing these things. Read on to find out how.

and your home are reference points. In a similar way, you might describe the position of a book by the shelf it is on. Or you might include a measurement and say that the book is 10 centimeters to the right of another book.

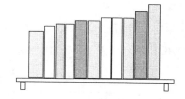

Position

Your teacher asks you where your book is. The place in which the book is located is its **position**. When you describe the position of an object, you include a reference point. A **reference point** is a place or object you use to describe position. For example, you might say that your book is on your desk, in your locker, or even at home. Your desk, your locker,

Key Terms

position—the location of an object

reference point—a place or object used to describe the position or relative motion of an object

motion—any change in the position of an object

relative motion—a change in the position of an object when compared with another object or location

distance—the length an object moves from a starting position

speed—the distance an object moves divided by the time during which it moves

Motion

If your book falls off your desk, you might say that it is in motion. An object is in **motion** if its position changes when compared with some reference point. The position of the falling book changes when compared with the desk and with the floor. Motion that is described by comparing the position of an object with a reference point is called **relative motion**. You would say that the object is moving *relative* to the reference point.

The most common reference point used to describe motion is the ground. Objects attached to the ground, such as trees or roadways, are also common reference points. The ground is not the only reference point, however. Suppose you are riding in a bus on your way to school. When compared with the trees, the road, and a nearby sidewalk, you are moving. If you use a different reference point, however, you may not be moving at all. Your position is not changing relative to the bus, the seat you are sitting in, or even a friend sitting next to you.

Did you know you are even moving when you are sitting at your desk or sleeping in bed? The reason is because you are on planet Earth. Earth travels in a path around the sun. In addition, it spins around like a top. So while you may not be moving when compared with the ground, you are moving very fast when you use the sun as a reference point.

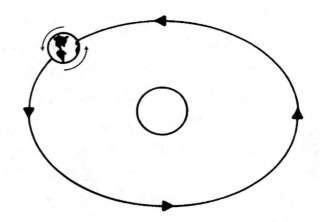

Distance

The change in an object's position is the **distance** it travels. In other words, distance describes how far an object has moved. Distance measures length. Therefore, when you describe distance, you must use units of length. A common unit of length that scientists use is the meter (m). A baseball bat is about 1 meter long. A football field is a little more than 90 meters long.

To measure longer distances, scientists use a unit known as a kilometer (km). There are 1,000 meters in 1 kilometer. The distance between New York City in New York and San Francisco in California is about 4,700 kilometers. The tallest mountain in the world, Mt. Everest, is almost 9 kilometers tall.

To measure shorter distances, scientists use centimeters (cm). There are 100 centimeters in 1 meter. An adult's fingernail has a width of about 1 centimeter. A new pencil is almost 20 centimeters long. A CD is about 12 centimeters across.

Scientists measure even shorter distances in millimeters (mm). There are 1,000 millimeters in 1 meter. A quarter is about 23 millimeters across.

1,000 meters = 1 kilometer
100 centimeters = 1 meter
1,000 millimeters = 1 meter

Speed

All motion is not the same. A snail inching its way along a leaf moves much more slowly than an eagle soaring through the air. Speed describes how fast or slow something moves. An object's **speed** measures its change in position during a specific amount of time.

To measure an object's speed, you need to know the distance it moved. You also need to know the time it took for the object to move that distance. For example, suppose a train is traveling on a track. It travels 75 kilometers during each hour. You would say that its speed is 75 kilometers per hour.

You can use the speed during 1 hour to predict how far an object will move over time. If the train travels 75 kilometers during 1 hour, you know that it travels twice as far during 2 hours, or 150 kilometers. How far will the train move during 3 hours at this speed? It will be 3 times as far as it moves in 1 hour, or 225 kilometers (3 × 75 kilometers = 225 kilometers).

Lesson 2   Review

Darken the circle by the best answer.

1. An object's location is also known as its
   - (A) distance.
   - (B) position.
   - (C) speed.
   - (D) reference.

2. How can you tell that an object is in motion?
   - (A) Its position changes.
   - (B) Its shape changes.
   - (C) Its size can be measured in different units.
   - (D) Its location remains the same over time.

3. When you measure distance, you are describing
   - (A) mass.
   - (B) speed.
   - (C) time.
   - (D) length.

4. The Colorado River carved out the Grand Canyon over time. What unit of measurement would be most useful for describing the length of the Colorado River?
   - (A) centimeters
   - (B) millimeters
   - (C) kilometers
   - (D) seconds

5. Two runners have a race around a track. The winner is the runner who
   - (A) moved at the fastest speed.
   - (B) ran the greatest distance.
   - (C) stayed in the same position.
   - (D) had the farthest reference point.

6. Which two measurements do you need to determine an object's speed?
   - (A) size and shape
   - (B) height and width
   - (C) distance and time
   - (D) mass and volume

Review (cont'd.)

7. Describe the position of your bed at home in at least three different ways.

_____

_____

_____

8. You are sitting in your seat in an airplane. The airplane is flying through the air. You are moving relative to some reference points, but not to others. Name an example of each type of reference point.

_____

_____

_____

9. An object is moving 10 kilometers each second. What is the object's speed? If its speed does not change, how far will it move in 20 seconds?

_____

_____

_____

Lesson 2, Review
Science 4, SV 9781419034329

Lesson 2   Position

In the space below, draw a simple map of the desks in your classroom. Write the names of the students who sit at each desk. When you are finished with your drawing, select three students in the class. On the lines provided, write a sentence describing the position of each student relative to the others. An example is provided for you.

Example: Susan sits behind Alissa, next to Chris, and in front of Chloe.

1. _____

_____

2. _____

_____

3. _____

_____

Lesson 2   **Position and Motion**

Unscramble each of the clue words.

Unscramble the letters that appear in ◯ **boxes to answer the riddle.**

1. EENEFRCRE OPNTI

2. DEPSE

3. POISOTNI

4. DETSINAC

5. LRTEIVEA NOTMOI

What describes what you are doing whether you are walking, riding, standing, sitting,

or sleeping? You are in ☐☐☐☐☐☐ .

Lesson 2

Breaking the Sound Barrier

Read the following passage. Then answer the questions that follow the passage.

Just as a ball rolling across a field moves at a certain speed, so do the sounds you hear. The speed of sound depends on the material through which it travels. For example, sound travels faster through metals than it does through liquids, such as water, or gases, such as air. The speed of sound also depends on temperature. Sounds travel faster through warm air than cold air.

On October 14, 1947, a pilot named Chuck Yeager took advantage of this fact. His goal was to travel faster than the speed of sound. This was known as breaking the sound barrier. The speed of sound at a specific temperature is known as Mach 1.

The temperature of air decreases as you rise through the atmosphere. Therefore, the speed of sound is slower up in the atmosphere than it is in the air near the ground. Flying in a vehicle known as the *Bell X-1*, Yeager flew high enough to make it possible for him to travel faster than Mach 1.

On October 15, 1997, a British vehicle broke the sound barrier on land. The vehicle was named the *Thrust SSC*, for supersonic car. Unlike ordinary cars, the *Thrust SSC* had two jet engines and needed a parachute to come to a stop.

Attempts to break the sound barrier were purposely made early in the morning. The reason was that at this time of day the temperature of air, and therefore the speed of sound, is at its lowest.

1. In which of the following materials would sound travel fastest?
   - (A) water in a swimming pool
   - (B) juice in a pitcher
   - (C) helium in a balloon
   - (D) copper in a wire

2. When Chuck Yeager broke the sound barrier, he
   - (A) carried a sound from one place to another.
   - (B) heard the quietest sound ever.
   - (C) traveled faster than sound.
   - (D) made the loudest sound ever.

3. Why was Yeager able to break the sound barrier high above the ground, but not on the ground?

Ⓐ Sound travels above the ground, but not near the ground.

Ⓑ The speed of sound is slower in the cold air high above the ground.

Ⓒ Sound travels more slowly near the ground than up in the atmosphere.

Ⓓ His airplane could travel faster higher in the atmosphere than it could in the air closer to the ground.

4. How would sound have changed if the *Thrust SSC* waited until noon to break the sound barrier?

Ⓐ The speed of sound would have been faster.

Ⓑ The speed of sound would have been slower.

Ⓒ The sound could not have traveled at that time of day.

Ⓓ The sound would have caused the air temperature to drop.

Lesson 2   Experiment: Investigating Motion

The speed of an object is the distance it moves divided by the time during which it moves that distance. In this activity, you will investigate how the speed of an object determines the distance it moves.

What You Will Need

several books of the same size
toy car
centimeter ruler
stopwatch
helper

Procedure

1. Place one book on the floor. Rest one end of another book at the top of the book. Put the other end of the book on the floor to make a ramp.

2. Place the car at the top of the ramp and let the car go. When the car reaches the bottom of the ramp, have your helper start the stopwatch.

3. Have your helper shout "Stop" when the stopwatch reads 3 seconds. When you hear this word, stop the car and hold it in place.

4. Use the ruler to measure the distance between the car and the bottom of the ramp. Record the distance in centimeters.

5. Stack another book on top of the book on the floor. Adjust the book acting as the ramp. Then repeat Steps 2 through 4.

6. Add another book to the stack and repeat Steps 2 through 4.

Experiment: Investigating Motion (cont'd.)

Analysis

Height of Ramp (Number of books in stack)	Distance Car Moved
1	
2	
3	

1. What is the purpose of adding books to the stack?

_____

_____

_____

2. How does adding books to the stack affect the speed of the car?

_____

_____

_____

_____

Conclusion

According to your results, how does the speed of an object affect the distance it moves in a given amount of time? How can you increase the distance an object moves in a given amount of time?

_____

_____

_____

_____

Lesson 3 Light, Heat, Electricity, and Magnetism

Things change around you all the time. You change positions by moving from one place to another. An oven changes food inside it by heating it. Electricity changes a light bulb by turning it on. The ability to cause things to change is known as **energy**.

Key Terms

energy—the ability to cause change

reflection—the bouncing of light off an object

refraction—the bending of light as it passes from one material to another at a slant

opaque—not allowing light to pass through

translucent—relating to an object that reflects some light, absorbs some light, and transmits some light

transparent—relating to an object that allows most of the light hitting it to pass through

thermal energy—the total energy of the particles in a sample of matter

heat—the transfer of thermal energy from a warmer object to a cooler one

conduction—the transfer of heat between particles of matter that are touching each other

convection—the transfer of heat by currents formed in liquids and gases

radiation—the transfer of heat without the use of matter

charge—a positive or negative characteristic of a particle that exerts an electric force on other charged particles

force—a push or a pull

electric field—the push or pull that surrounds a charged particle

static electricity—charge that does not flow

electric current—the flow of electric charge

circuit—a path through which electric current can flow

magnet—an object that attracts materials, such as metals, to it

magnetic pole—a region of a magnet where the magnetic effects are strongest

electromagnet—a wire carrying electric current that is twisted into loops and wrapped around an iron core

generator—a device that uses a changing magnetic field to produce electric current

There are different kinds of energy. One type of energy is light energy. Light makes it possible for you to see the things around you. What are some things that produce light? Some sources of light are found in nature, such as the sun and the stars. Other sources of light are made by people, such as light bulbs.

How Light Behaves

When you look in a mirror, you see one way that light behaves. You can see yourself in a mirror because light that hits the mirror bounces back to your eye. The bouncing of light off an object is known as **reflection**.

A mirror produces a clear picture, or image. A clear image is produced whenever light is reflected off a smooth surface. You might also see a clear image in a calm lake or a shiny material. A rough surface, such as a crumpled sheet of foil, can also reflect light. However, it will produce a fuzzy image because the light is reflected off in many directions.

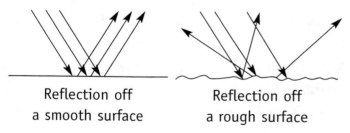

Reflection off a smooth surface   Reflection off a rough surface

Not all surfaces reflect light. Some surfaces allow light to pass through them. A clear window, for example, allows light to pass through it. When light passes from one type of matter to another, its speed changes. When light passes from air into the glass and water of a fish tank, the light slows down. If the light hits the new type of matter straight on, it changes speed and goes straight through it. If the light hits the matter at a slant, part of the light will change speed before the other part. This causes the light to bend. The bending of light when it moves from one type of matter to another is called **refraction**. Refraction explains why objects, such as straws or flower stems, look bent in water.

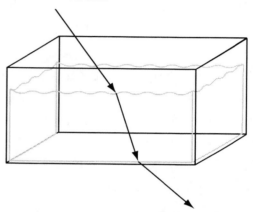

Some objects neither reflect nor refract light. Instead, they absorb light. To absorb means to take in or stop light. A black wall, for example, absorbs the light that strikes it.

The type of object determines what happens to the light that reaches it. An **opaque** object reflects or absorbs all of the light that reaches it. A refrigerator door is an opaque object. A **translucent** object reflects some light and absorbs some light. It allows any remaining light to pass through it. The light that passes through a translucent object does not produce a clear image. Instead, it makes a blurry or fuzzy image. Many shower doors produce this type of image. A **transparent**

Lesson 3, Light, Heat, Electricity, and Magnetism
Science 4, SV 9781419034329

object does not reflect or absorb much light. It allows most light to pass through it. A clear window is an example of a transparent object.

What Is Heat?

You know that a cup of hot chocolate is warmer than a glass of cold chocolate milk. The reason has to do with the particles that make up matter. All matter is made up of smaller particles. These particles are constantly moving in all directions. The total energy that the particles have is called **thermal energy**.

What happens when you drop an ice cube into a warm glass of water? Over time, the ice cube melts and the water becomes colder. Why? When a warm substance is near a cooler substance, thermal energy moves from the warmer substance to the cooler one. The transfer of thermal energy is called **heat**. In the case of the ice and water, the water is warmer than the ice cube. Heat is therefore transferred from the water to the ice cube.

When a substance gives up thermal energy, it becomes colder. This is why the water becomes colder. When a substance gains thermal energy, it becomes warmer. This is why the ice cube melts.

thermal energy

Heat Transfer

Heat can be transferred between objects in three different ways. They are conduction, convection, and radiation.

Conduction Perhaps you have noticed that a spoon placed in a bowl of hot soup becomes warm. Heat is transferred from the hot soup to the cold spoon by conduction. During **conduction**, thermal energy moves between particles of matter that are touching each other.

Convection Energy transfer in a liquid or a gas is known as **convection**. The particles in liquids and gases can move more freely than those in a solid. Look at the water in the pot on page 33. The water at the bottom of the pot becomes hot from the coils on the stove. The hot particles move faster and farther apart. In other words, they become less dense. The water above it is colder and denser. As a result, the colder water sinks and the warmer water is pushed upward. The cold water that is now at the bottom of the pot is then heated. As it warms up, it becomes less dense and the process happens again. The water begins to move in a circular pattern known as a convection current.

Radiation One form of heat transfer does not involve matter. The movement of heat without the use of matter is **radiation**. Heat is transferred from the sun by means of radiation. Even though radiation does not require matter, it can occur through matter. Radiation is how heat is transferred from a campfire to your hands.

Electricity

The particles that make up matter are made of even smaller particles. Some of those smaller particles have a property known as electric **charge**. A charge can either be positive ($+$) or negative ($-$).

Even though matter contains charges, many objects do not have an overall charge. The reason is that the number of positive charges is equal to the number of negative charges. As a result, the charges cancel out. The object is said to be neutral.

Some objects are not neutral. In these objects, the number of positive charges is not equal to the number of negative charges. If the object has more negative charges than positive charges, its overall charge is negative. If the object has more positive charges than negative charges, the overall charge is positive.

Electric Force

Charged objects exert an electric force on one another. A **force** is a push or a pull. If the charges are the same, the objects push one another apart (repel). If the charges are different, the objects pull each other together (attract).

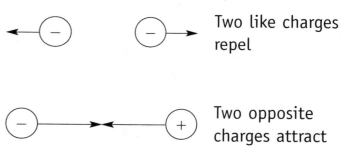

Two like charges repel

Two opposite charges attract

Each charge is surrounded by an **electric field**. A charged particle that comes into the electric field of another charge will experience an electric force. The diagrams below use arrows to show the electric fields around charges. The arrows point in the direction in which a positive charge would be moved.

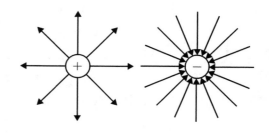

Lesson 3, Light, Heat, Electricity, and Magnetism
Science 4, SV 9781419034329

Types of Electricity

The charge that stays on an object is called **static electricity**. The word *static* means "not moving." The flow of electric charge is called **electric current**. Charges need a path to follow. A **circuit** is a path through which electric current can flow. A simple circuit is made up of a source of electric energy, such as a battery. It also contains a material through which electric current can flow, such as a metal wire. A light bulb or other device in the circuit will be controlled by the current. A switch can be used to turn the current on and off.

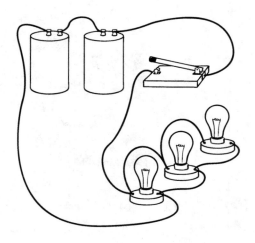

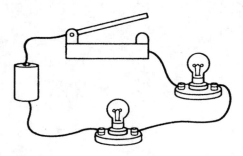

Series Circuit A circuit in which there is only one path for the current is called a series circuit. In the series circuit above, current travels from the battery to the bulb and back to the battery. If any part of the circuit is broken or removed, no current will move in the circuit. So if one of the bulbs burns out, current will not flow to the other bulb.

Parallel Circuit A circuit in which there is more than one path for the current to flow through is called a parallel circuit. In the parallel circuit at the top of the page, current travels through each of the paths with a bulb. If one of the bulbs burns out, current will still travel through the other path.

Magnetism

Do you have a magnet on your refrigerator or locker? A **magnet** is an object that attracts certain materials to it, such as iron or steel. Magnets come in different shapes. A common magnet is in the form of a bar. Other magnets are shaped like horseshoes or flat discs. Some magnets even occur naturally in rocks called lodestone.

Magnets have two regions called **magnetic poles**. One pole is known as the north pole and the other is the south pole. The diagram shows that the poles of a bar magnet are at the ends. The effects of a magnet are strongest at the poles.

Magnetic Force

Much like the electric field around an electric charge, a magnet is surrounded by a magnetic field. When one magnet comes into the magnetic field of another, it is

Lesson 3, Light, Heat, Electricity, and Magnetism
Science 4, SV 9781419034329

pushed or pulled by a magnetic force. If two poles that are the same come near each other, they push each other apart. Two north poles will push each other apart. Two south poles will also push each other apart.

If two poles that are different come near each other, they will pull each other together. A north pole of one magnet will pull the south pole of another magnet toward it.

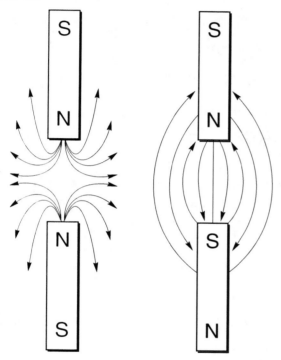

Electricity and Magnetism

When an electric current moves through a wire, it makes a magnetic field. In fact, the magnetic field around a wire carrying electric current looks much like that of a bar magnet. The magnetic field, however, is much weaker than it is around a bar magnet. If the wire is wound into loops, the magnetic field becomes stronger. The more loops that are made, the stronger the field is. If a material such as iron is placed inside the loops, the field becomes even stronger. A wire wrapped around an iron core is called an **electromagnet**.

Electromagnets are useful because they can be turned on and off. When the electric current is turned on, the electromagnet produces a magnetic field. As soon as the current is turned off, the electromagnet stops producing a magnetic field. This makes electromagnets useful for lifting and then letting go of objects. The size and strength of the electromagnet can be changed for different objects. Some electromagnets lift tiny objects inside computers. Other electromagnets lift objects as large as cars.

Just as electricity can produce a magnetic field, a magnetic field can produce electricity. In a device called a **generator**, the direction of a magnetic field is constantly changed. This produces an electric current. The electric current from large generators is sent to homes and businesses. It is this electricity you use whenever you plug a device into an electrical outlet in the wall.

Lesson 3

Review

Darken the circle by the best answer.

1. Which of these is the best definition of energy?
   - (A) the bouncing of light off an object
   - (B) the pull between two objects
   - (C) the ability to cause change
   - (D) the heating of a cold object

2. Which of these happens to light when it is refracted?
   - (A) It is bent.
   - (B) It bounces off an object.
   - (C) It is absorbed.
   - (D) It is destroyed.

3. Which of these is a transparent object?
   - (A) textbook
   - (B) soccer ball
   - (C) wood floor
   - (D) sheet of plastic wrap

4. Air near Earth's surface is heated and rises. Colder air sinks into its place and is then heated as well. The cycle then happens again. This type of heating is known as
   - (A) convection.
   - (B) conduction.
   - (C) radiation.
   - (D) thermation.

5. Which two particles will be pulled together when placed near each other?
   - (A) two positive particles
   - (B) two negative particles
   - (C) two neutral particles
   - (D) a positive particle and a negative particle

6. Which part of a circuit is a source of electric energy?
   - (A) switch
   - (B) wire
   - (C) battery
   - (D) lightbulb

NAME ______________________________ DATE ______________

Review (cont'd.)

7. The parts of a magnet where its effects are strongest are known as

(A) charges.

(B) poles.

(C) switches.

(D) batteries.

8. Jarret brought a snowball into the house. He left it on the kitchen counter. How does heat flow between the snowball and the counter? What will eventually happen to the snowball?

____

____

____

9. What is an electromagnet? What are two advantages of an electromagnet?

____

____

____

Lesson 3

Describing Forms of Energy

Circle the following words in the puzzle below. They may appear horizontally, vertically, or diagonally.

CHARGE

CIRCUIT

CONDUCTION

CONVECTION

ENERGY

FORCE

GENERATOR

HEAT

MAGNET

OPAQUE

RADIATION

REFLECTION

REFRACTION

THERMAL

TRANSLUCENT

TRANSPARENT

```
B  R  N  T  R  L  M  M  V  B  O  E  E  N  G
E  E  O  Z  R  A  E  H  N  X  P  R  G  O  E
N  F  I  T  B  A  D  Q  P  S  A  V  R  I  N
O  L  T  X  E  G  N  I  S  B  Q  Q  A  T  E
I  E  C  E  W  N  D  S  A  B  U  Y  H  C  R
T  C  A  M  V  Q  G  T  P  T  E  T  C  U  A
C  T  R  A  R  E  H  A  D  A  I  Z  Z  D  T
E  I  F  S  M  E  V  M  M  N  R  O  O  N  O
V  O  E  K  R  E  N  E  R  G  Y  E  N  O  R
N  N  R  M  T  I  U  C  R  I  C  N  N  C  F
O  E  A  E  M  W  X  G  B  V  W  Z  L  T  I
C  L  C  H  T  R  A  N  S  L  U  C  E  N  T
T  K  F  R  E  Z  Z  H  A  Q  L  D  B  Y  G
O  K  N  B  O  A  U  Z  Z  G  R  H  M  S  O
B  J  T  Q  H  F  T  D  D  T  P  R  M  X  O
```

Lesson 3   **Heat Transfer**

Each of the diagrams shows an example of how heat is transferred. On the line by each one, write the type of heat transfer. Then describe one more example of this type of heat transfer.

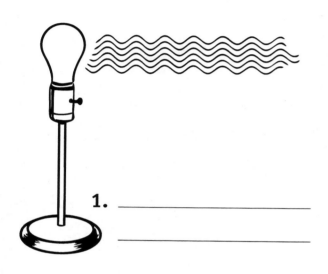

1. _____

_____

2. _____

_____

3. _____

_____

Lesson 3, Heat Transfer
Science 4, SV 9781419034329

Lesson 3   Electric Circuits

Diagrams similar to the ones below are used to represent circuits. Write the name of each part of the circuits on the lines shown. Then decide which of these is a series circuit and which of these is a parallel circuit. Write the type of circuit on the line beside each diagram.

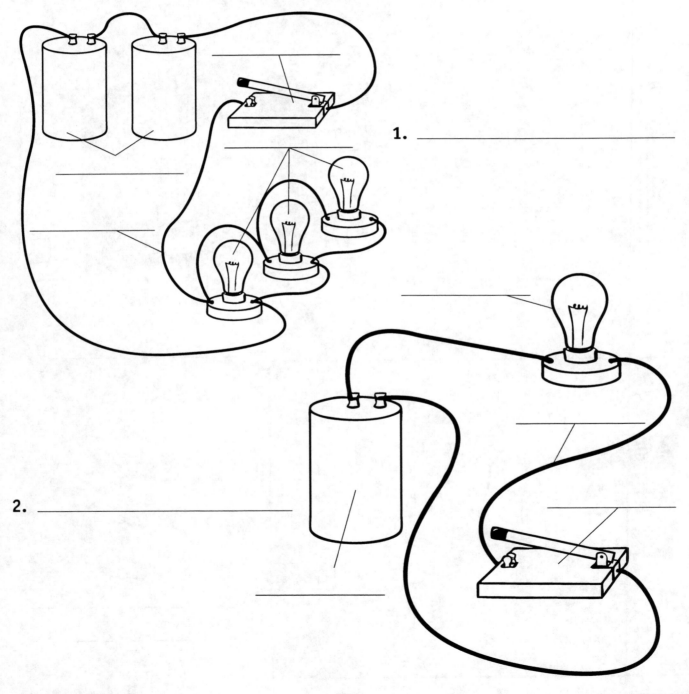

1. _____

2. _____

Lesson 3, Electric Circuits
Science 4, SV 9781419034329

Lesson 3   Comparing Forms of Energy

Fill in the key term that completes each sentence. Choose from the words below.

charge	circuit	electromagnet
energy	force	generator
heat	reflection	refraction
transparent		

1. Light is one type of _____.

2. During the process of _____, light bends as it enters a new material.

3. A(n) _____ uses a magnetic field to produce an electric current.

4. _____ is the transfer of thermal energy.

5. When you push on a door, you exert a(n) _____ on it.

6. The process through which light bounces off an object is called

_____.

7. Electric current needs a(n) _____ in order to flow.

8. Particles of matter can have a positive or negative electric

_____.

9. The windshield of a school bus is a(n) _____ object.

10. You can make a(n) _____ by wrapping the wire from an electric circuit around an iron core.

Lesson 3   Experiment: Investigating Reflection

Light is reflected from a mirror. However, it is not always reflected in the same direction. The direction in which light bounces off a mirror depends on the direction in which it hits the mirror. In this experiment, you will use this information to make light go around an object.

What You Will Need

3 small mirrors
clay or dough
small flashlight
shoe box
index card
marker

Procedure

1. Draw an X on an index card. Use a small ball of clay to stand the card up on a desk, floor, or other flat surface.

2. Place the shoebox about 25 centimeters in front of the card.

3. Arrange the three mirrors so that a beam of light shined on the first mirror will reflect off the other two mirrors and reach the card with the X. The first mirror must be on the side of the shoe box opposite the index card. Use balls of clay to stand up the mirrors.

4. Dim the lights in the room. Turn on the flashlight and test your arrangement of mirrors. If the beam of light does not reach the card, rearrange the mirrors until it does. It may take you several arrangements.

Experiment: Investigating Reflection (cont'd.)

Analysis

In the space below, draw a diagram showing the arrangement of mirrors. Use a straight line to show how light travels from the flashlight to the index card.

Conclusion

1. What happens if you shine light straight at a mirror?

_____

_____

2. How did you have to shine the light at each mirror so it would bounce to the next mirror?

_____

_____

Lesson 4 Characteristics of Organisms

What comes to mind when you think of living things? Perhaps you imagine a bird flying from one tree to another. Maybe you think of dogs, cats, and even people. You might even consider plants, such as trees. But did you know that there are millions of types of living things that you can't even see without a microscope? Living things, also known as **organisms**, come in many different shapes and sizes.

Organisms Are Made Up of Cells

No matter how different they are, all organisms share several characteristics.

All organisms are made up of cells. A **cell** is the basic unit of living things.

Some organisms are made up of only one cell. Bacteria are one-celled organisms. Other organisms are made up of more than one cell. Large organisms, such as people, are made up of millions of cells.

In these organisms, different cells perform special jobs. Groups of similar cells make up **tissues**. A group of tissues that work together is called an **organ**. The heart, stomach, and lungs are examples of organs. Organs that work together to perform a task make up an **organ system**. Your digestive system is made up of organs such as the stomach and

Key Terms

organism—a living thing

cell—the basic unit of living things

tissue—a group of cells that work together to perform a task

organ—a group of tissues that work together to perform a task

organ system—a group of organs that work together to perform a task

organelle—a part of a cell that performs a task the cell needs to survive

reproduction—the process through which organisms make more organisms like themselves

photosynthesis—the process through which an organism uses light energy to change carbon dioxide and water into food and oxygen

cellular respiration—the process through which an organism uses oxygen to release energy stored in food

intestines. They work together to break down food for your body to use.

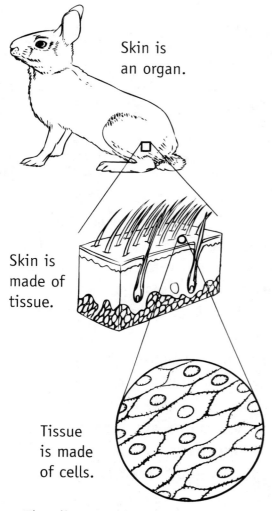

Skin is an organ.

Skin is made of tissue.

Tissue is made of cells.

The diagrams below show an example of a cell from an animal and a cell from a plant. Notice that each cell contains smaller parts. These parts are called organelles. An **organelle** is a part of a cell that performs a task the cell needs to survive.

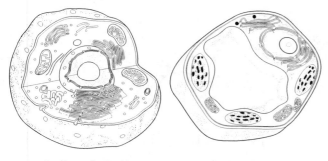

Animal Cell   Plant Cell

Organisms Respond to Their Environment

When your alarm goes off in the morning, you wake up and know it is time to get up for school. Waking up is the way that you respond to the alarm. Organisms respond to many different signals in their environment. Some trees lose their leaves in the fall. These trees respond to changes in the amount of light they receive. They also respond to changes in temperature. Sounds, light, and temperature are just some of the changes that cause organisms to respond. Organisms can also respond to changes in chemicals, tastes, and touch.

Organisms Are Able to Reproduce

In a process known as **reproduction**, organisms make more organisms like themselves. Every single living organism does not have to reproduce. However, organisms must be able to reproduce if they are to continue living on Earth. Think about what would happen if the eagles that are alive today were unable to produce more eagles. When these eagles die out, there would be no new eagles to take their place. As a result, there would no longer be any eagles on Earth. Instead, some eagles do reproduce. When the young eagles grow up, they reproduce as well. In a continuous cycle such as this, organisms continue to live on Earth.

Lesson 4, Characteristics of Organisms
Science 4, SV 9781419034329

Organisms Grow and Develop

You began your life as a tiny baby. Over time, you grew into the person you are today. You will continue to grow until you become an adult. At some point in their lives, all organisms grow.

Your growth resulted from the dividing of cells. You started as a single cell that divided into two cells. Those two cells each divided into two cells. This process continued to make the millions of cells in your body today. Even when you are fully grown, cells in your body will continue to divide. They do this to replace any cells that have become worn out or damaged.

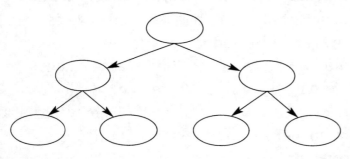

For organisms made up of only one cell, growth is a bit more simple. Growth for one-celled organisms usually means that the cell becomes larger. There is a limit to how large cells can become. Cells take in the materials they need. They

also get rid of any waste materials they produce. If a cell becomes too large, it will not be able to get enough nutrients or get rid of wastes fast enough. This is why most cells remain small.

Organisms Share Certain Needs

All organisms must have their needs met in order to survive. Most organisms share similar needs. These include the need for energy, water, temperature in a certain range, air, and a place to live.

Energy The processes that occur in cells use energy. Recall that energy is the ability to cause change. In order to survive, organisms need energy. Many organisms, such as plants, get the energy they need from sunlight. In a process known as **photosynthesis**, plants and some other organisms use the energy of sunlight to make food. The energy from the sun is changed into a form that is stored in the food. To do this, plants change carbon dioxide and water into food and oxygen. They store the food in their tissues until they need it.

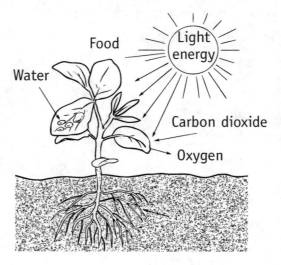

When plants need energy, they break down some of the stored food. In a process known as **cellular respiration**, food is broken down to release energy that can be used by cells. Cellular respiration happens only when oxygen is present.

Animals and many other organisms do not conduct photosynthesis. How do organisms that do not conduct photosynthesis get energy? Some organisms eat plants. When they do so, these organisms take in the energy stored in the plants. Like the plants, these organisms use the energy they need and store any extra energy. Zebras, cows, and panda bears are some of the many organisms that feed directly on plants.

Other organisms eat organisms that ate plants. When a lion eats a zebra, the energy stored in the zebra is passed on to the lion.

Water Most of the processes that take place in cells need water. One reason is that substances break apart, or dissolve, in water. Think about adding a powdered drink mix to a pitcher of water. The drink mix dissolves in the water to make a drink that tastes good. In a similar way, many of the materials that cells need must dissolve in water in order to be useful.

Another way that water is important to living things is in carrying materials. Water can flow from one place to another much as it does in a stream or river. In organisms, water makes up a large portion of fluids. In humans, for example, water is a large part of blood. Blood carries materials, such as oxygen, throughout the body. Water is also a part of the fluids that help the body break down foods into particles the body can use.

The Right Temperature Organisms need a certain temperature range in order to survive. Some organisms, such as dogs, keep their inside temperature about the same all the time. If the outside temperature becomes cold, these organisms can make changes to become warmer. One way is to change energy they have stored into thermal energy. Thermal energy helps to keep the organism warm. Have you every shivered on a cold day? Shivering is another way that your body keeps warm.

The opposite is also true. If the outside temperature becomes too warm, these organisms make changes to cool off. Dogs breathe through their mouths. This process, known as panting, helps release heat. People can sweat. When a person sweats, a liquid on the skin changes into a gas and enters the air. As it does so, it transfers heat away from the body.

Not all organisms can control their temperature in this way. Organisms such as lizards take on the temperature of their surroundings. When these organisms become cool, they can move to warm surroundings. This is why you might see a lizard or other reptile basking on a hot rock or other surface. When these organisms become too warm, they can move to cooler surroundings. Some move to shady places. Others burrow into the ground. Still others open their mouths to cool off.

Air You may not think about it much, but you are breathing all the time. With each breath, you take in oxygen from the air. Your cells use this oxygen to release the energy they need. When you breathe out, you release carbon dioxide that your body does not need. Organisms that conduct photosynthesis also need air. However, unlike you, they take in carbon dioxide and release oxygen.

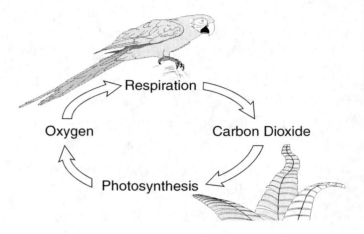

A Place to Live All organisms need a place to live. This place not only gives the organism a spot to live in, but it also supplies the things it needs. Some organisms need only a small space. Others need a much larger space. This is one reason why it is so important to protect the places where animals live.

Lesson 4   Review

Darken the circle by the best answer.

1. Which is the most basic unit of life?
   - (A) cell
   - (B) tissue
   - (C) organ
   - (D) system

2. Which of these is not necessarily a characteristic of all living things?
   - (A) They are made of cells.
   - (B) They respond to their environments.
   - (C) They need energy.
   - (D) They are green.

3. Which of these organisms conducts photosynthesis?
   - (A) fish
   - (B) tree
   - (C) human
   - (D) tiger

4. Which of these happens during cellular respiration?
   - (A) An organism stores energy in food.
   - (B) An organism eats an organism that has made food.
   - (C) An organism breaks down food to release energy.
   - (D) An organism captures the energy of sunlight.

5. Which of these actions will help keep an organism warm?
   - (A) dog panting
   - (B) person shivering
   - (C) frog burying itself in mud
   - (D) person sweating

6. Which of the following materials do plants need from the air to conduct photosynthesis?
   - (A) carbon dioxide
   - (B) food
   - (C) oxygen
   - (D) space

Review (cont'd.)

7. Do both animals and plants conduct photosynthesis? Do both animals and plants conduct cellular respiration? Explain your answers.

_____

_____

_____

_____

_____

_____

8. Many substances can dissolve in water. Why is this important to living things?

_____

_____

_____

_____

_____

_____

Lesson 4

Types of Cells

Look at the plant and animal cells shown below. Make a list of the parts, or organelles, in each cell. Circle any organelles that are in one cell but not the other cell.

An Animal Cell

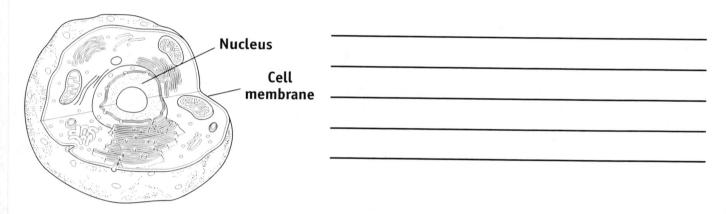

Nucleus

Cell membrane

_____

_____

_____

_____

_____

A Plant Cell

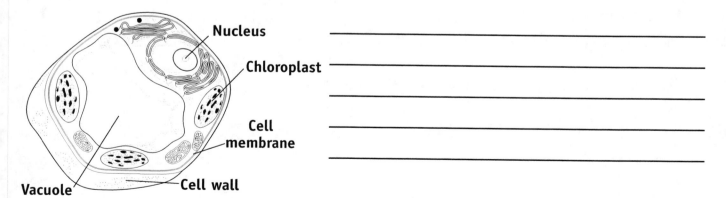

Nucleus

Chloroplast

Cell membrane

Vacuole

Cell wall

_____

_____

_____

_____

Lesson 4 Prefixes

A prefix is a letter or group of letters placed at the beginning of a word to change its meaning. Knowing the meaning of a prefix can help you to understand many words you read in science.

The box below gives the meanings of two prefixes from this lesson. Use these meanings to write a definition for the underlined word in each sentence below.

Prefix	Meaning
photo-	light
re-	back or again

1. The water plant conducts <u>photosynthesis</u>.

_____

_____

2. The flowers of some plants are used in <u>reproduction</u>.

_____

_____

3. Sally had to <u>rewrite</u> her homework.

_____

_____

4. Thomas had to <u>rewind</u> the tape after the movie.

_____

_____

5. The teacher took a <u>photograph</u> of the class.

_____

_____

Lesson 4

Describing Living Things

Vocabulary terms from this lesson have been broken up into separate boxes. The boxes are out of order. Unscramble the boxes to reveal the terms. Rewrite the letters in order in the spaces provided.

1. | O N | C E L | R E S | A R | L U L | P I R | A T I |

2. | S S | U E | T I |

3. | G A N E | L L E | O R |

4. | R O D | R E P | I O N | U C T |

5. | H E S | I S | T O S | Y N T | P H O |

6. | A N I | O R G | S M |

Lesson 4   Discovering Cells

Read the following passage. At the end is a list of phrases relating to the passage, along with a Venn diagram. In the circle on the left, write the phrases that apply only to Robert Hooke. In circle on the right, write the phrases that apply only to Anton van Leeuwenhoek. In the center where the circles overlap, write the phrases that apply to both scientists.

In the 1600s, a scientist named Robert Hooke developed one of the first microscopes. A microscope is a tool that a person can use to look at very small objects. In 1665, Hooke used his microscope to study a piece of cork. He saw that the cork was made up of tiny, empty sections. These sections looked like rooms in a building where monks lived. Because these rooms were called *cells*, he gave this name to the sections in the cork.

The cork that Hooke studied was not alive. Anton van Leeuwenhoek was the first person to look at living cells. Like Hooke, Leeuwenhoek made a simple microscope. However, he looked at pond water. In 1678, he described the water as being filled with tiny living organisms. He named them *animacules*, which means "tiny animals." The tiny living things that can be seen through a microscope are now known as microorganisms.

Used a microscope   Worked in the 1600s
Made up the name "cells"   Saw living cells
Studied pond water   Studied cork

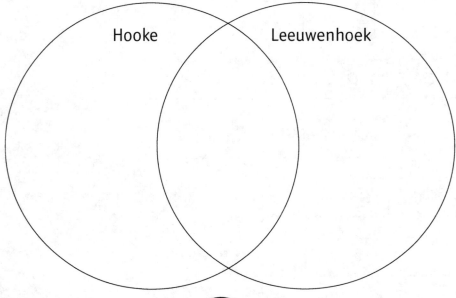

Lesson 4

Experiment: Getting Too Close

Some plants make chemicals that keep other plants from growing too close to them. In this activity, you will test how close plants can grow to sweet potato plants.

What You Will Need

6 small flowerpots
soil
seeds (sweet potato, radish, bean)
water
marker

Procedure

1. Fill 6 small flowerpots partway with soil. Label the pots "1," "2," "3," "4," "5," and "6."

2. In Pot 1, plant 10 radish seeds.

3. In Pot 2, plant 2 sweet potato seeds.

4. In Pot 3, plant 10 radish seeds and 2 sweet potato seeds.

5. In Pot 4, plant 10 bean seeds.

6. In Pot 5, plant 10 bean seeds and 10 radish seeds.

7. In Pot 6, plant 10 bean seeds and 2 sweet potato seeds.

8. Set the pots on a windowsill and water all of the pots every day. Observe how the plants in each pot grow. Keep notes of your observations.

Analysis

1. Why did you put only one type of seed in some of the pots?

_____

_____

_____

Experiment: Getting Too Close (cont'd.)

2. Why did you plant beans and radishes together?

_____

_____

_____

_____

Conclusion

What happened to the seeds planted with sweet potato seeds? Why?

_____

_____

_____

_____

_____

Lesson 5 Life Cycles of Organisms

You're out for a ride on your bicycle. Think about what happens to your wheels as you ride. They spin in a circle over and over again. A series of events that occurs over and over again is called a **cycle**. Many cycles occur in nature. The moon travels around Earth in a cycle. Earth has a cycle of seasons. Dark areas called sunspots appear on the sun in a regular cycle.

Organisms also go through a cycle of life. The **life cycle** of an organism describes the changes that happen from the time it is born until it dies. Although the life of the organism ends, it is called a cycle because the organism might reproduce during its life. In this way, the cycle begins all over again.

Metamorphosis

The life cycle of some organisms is described as metamorphosis. During **metamorphosis**, the body and the behavior of an organism change.

Sometimes metamorphosis means that an organism will live in a different place as it changes. One organism that undergoes such a metamorphosis is a frog.

Frogs begin as eggs released into water. The eggs hatch into tadpoles. A tadpole is similar to a fish in that it has gills. The gills let the tadpole breathe in the water. The tadpole grows quickly. It feeds on smaller organisms in the water, such as algae. Over time, legs form on the tadpole's body. Its tail becomes smaller and finally disappears altogether.

Key Terms

cycle—a series of events that occurs over and over again

life cycle—the changes that occur to an organism between birth and death

metamorphosis—changes in the body and behavior of an organism

zygote—the single cell that begins the human life cycle

germinate—to sprout, as a plant seedling

spore—a cell that can grow into a new plant

At the same time, the systems inside the tadpole change. For example, the tadpole develops lungs so it can breathe outside of the water. When all of the changes are complete, the tadpole has become a frog. The frog then lives on land instead of in the water. The frog goes back into the water when it reproduces. This begins the cycle all over again.

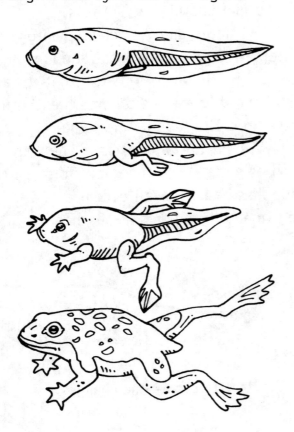

Insects also undergo metamorphosis. There are two types of insect metamorphosis: incomplete and complete. The type depends on the insect.

Incomplete Metamorphosis Grasshoppers, dragonflies, and cockroaches undergo incomplete metamorphosis. This type of metamorphosis involves three stages: egg, nymph, and adult. You can see from the diagram that the egg hatches

into the nymph, which looks much like the adult without wings.

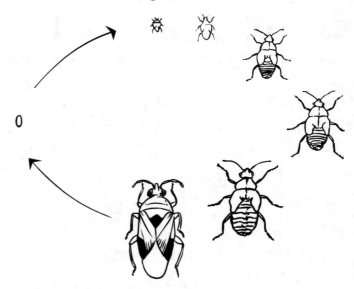

Complete Metamorphosis Butterflies, beetles, and bees undergo complete metamorphosis. This type of metamorphosis involves four stages: egg, larva, pupa, and adult. Eggs hatch into larvae, which look like worms. A larva then becomes a pupa. The pupa is protected by a covering. The pupa does not eat or move, but it changes a lot. Eventually, the adult insect forms.

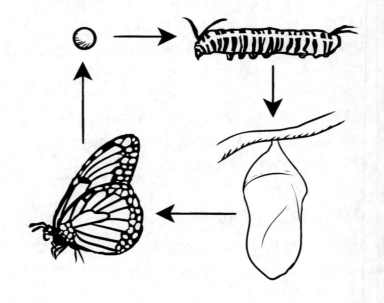

The Human Life Cycle

The human life cycle begins with a single cell called a **zygote**. The zygote divides over and over again until it forms a ball of cells called an embryo. As the cells continue to divide, the embryo grows into a fetus. After 9 months of development inside the mother's body, a baby is born.

The first 2 years of life are known as infancy. During this period of time, a baby grows in size. The shape and features of the baby develop as well. At the same time, the baby becomes able to control its movements.

The period of time between 2 and 12 years of age is known as childhood. Children continue to grow and develop. After age 12, a child gradually becomes an adult. This period is known as adolescence. After adolescence comes adulthood. A period known as aging begins at around 30 years of age.

Plant Life Cycles

If you have ever planted seeds in a garden or pot, you know the first stage of the life cycles of flowering plants. Plants that have flowers begin as seeds. If the seed gets the conditions it needs, it will **germinate**, or sprout. A seedling will grow. With the right amount of light,

water, air, and soil, the seedling will grow into an adult plant.

Some other plants begin as seeds that do not come from flowers. Pine trees are an example of this type of plant. Perhaps you have seen a pine cone. Seeds are produced in pine cones. When the seeds are ready to germinate, the scales of the cone open. This lets the wind blow the seeds away. Some of the seeds will land in places that make it possible for them to grow into seedlings.

Many plants do not produce seeds at all. These plants make **spores**, which are cells that can grow into new plants. The life cycles of these plants last for two generations. This means that one generation of plants makes male and female cells that join together to form a new plant. This new plant then makes spores. The spores grow into a plant that makes male and female cells. This cycle continues over and over again.

Lesson 5   Review

Darken the circle by the best answer.

1. Which shape would best represent a cycle?

   (A) slanted line

   (B) circle

   (C) flat line

   (D) zigzag

2. Where does a frog live during its life cycle?

   (A) It moves from air to land.

   (B) It moves from land to trees.

   (C) It moves from water to land.

   (D) It moves from outdoors to indoors.

3. Which sentence about incomplete metamorphosis is true?

   (A) It is made up of four stages.

   (B) Only large animals undergo this type of change.

   (C) Spores are one of the stages.

   (D) The second stage looks much like the adult stage.

4. How does a human zygote become an embryo?

   (A) It divides over and over again.

   (B) It takes in nutrients and changes shape.

   (C) It grows larger during a period called infancy.

   (D) It joins with cells from other organisms.

5. What happens when a seed germinates?

   (A) It makes flowers.

   (B) It gets sick.

   (C) It dies.

   (D) It sprouts.

6. The seeds of pine trees are produced in

   (A) spores.

   (B) flowers.

   (C) cones.

   (D) tadpoles.

Review (cont'd.)

7. How is incomplete metamorphosis different from complete metamorphosis?

_____

_____

_____

_____

_____

_____

8. In what way is a human zygote similar to the seed of a flowering plant?

_____

_____

_____

Lesson 5   Growing Up

Write a paragraph describing how you have changed since you were a baby. Include details such as how you looked, what you have done, and where you lived. For example, your hair color may have changed since you were little. Or the things you enjoy may have changed as you have grown.

When you are finished, draw one line under the main idea of your paragraph. Draw two lines under any supporting details.

_____

_____

_____

_____

_____

_____

_____

_____

_____

_____

_____

_____

_____

_____

_____

_____

_____

_____

_____

Lesson 5   Describing Change

Write a key term to complete each sentence. Choose from the words below.

germinate	metamorphosis	spores	zygote	cycle

1. The change from day to night and back again is a continuous

_____.

2. A _____ is the single cell from which a human develops.

3. Some plants make _____, which are single cells that can grow into plants.

4. A tadpole changes into an adult frog during _____.

5. A seed will _____ if it gets the sunlight, soil, and water it needs.

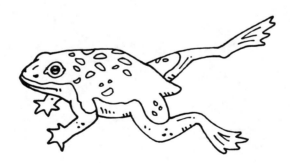

Lesson 5   Insect Life Cycles

The diagram shows the life cycle of a fly. Decide what type of metamorphosis happens to the fly. On the lines below, write a sentence or two explaining the reasons for your decision.

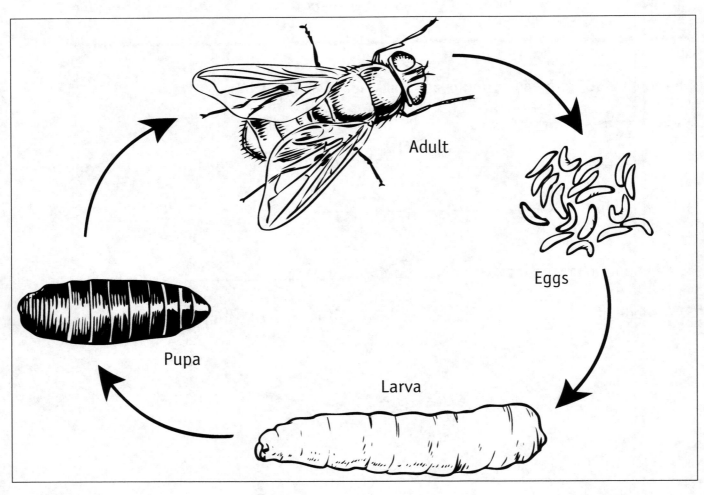

Stages in Life Cycle of Flies

_____

_____

_____

_____

         Science 4, SV 9781419034329

Lesson 5
The Monarch Butterfly

Read the following passage. Then answer the questions that follow the passage.

If you see a caterpillar walking along a milkweed plant, you might be looking at a young monarch butterfly. These insects begin as tiny eggs that change into caterpillars. In time, the young caterpillar is protected in a structure called a pupa. Finally, a beautiful monarch butterfly comes out.

Different types of monarch butterflies are found wherever milkweed plants grow. What is so special about the milkweed plant? Female butterflies lay their eggs on the bottoms of the leaves of a milkweed plant. Between 3 and 12 days, the eggs hatch into larvae. The larvae eat the milkweed leaves. This is the only food they can eat.

Milkweed has poisons that the butterfly eats. The poisons do not hurt the butterfly. Instead, they are dangerous to any animals that might eat the butterfly. In nature, bright colors in an organism often warn other organisms about poisons. This is why monarch butterflies are a bright orange color.

Another interesting fact about monarch butterflies is that they fly long distances every year. In the fall, butterflies from northern places fly south where the temperatures are warmer. Some butterflies travel up to 3,000 kilometers! They are known to gather in certain places in Mexico and California.

The Monarch Butterfly (cont'd.)

1. On which of the following plants does a monarch butterfly grow up?

   (A) rosebush

   (B) pine tree

   (C) milkweed

   (D) grass

2. Which statement about the development of a monarch butterfly is true?

   (A) It goes through incomplete metamorphosis.

   (B) It goes through complete metamorphosis.

   (C) It is born in its adult form.

   (D) It is born as a small butterfly that grows larger.

3. Which clue might tell a bird that a monarch butterfly is poisonous?

   (A) It has a bright orange color.

   (B) It is small in size.

   (C) It flies long distances.

   (D) It does not like cold weather.

4. Why do monarch butterflies travel to Mexico and California in the fall?

   (A) to find food

   (B) to find water

   (C) to reproduce

   (D) to get warm

Lesson 5

Experiment: The Parts of a Flower

Some plants need flowers to reproduce. In this activity, you will look at the parts of a flower.

What You Will Need

a large lily or other flower
black paper
white paper
toothpick
magnifying glass
apple

CAUTION: Adult help required.

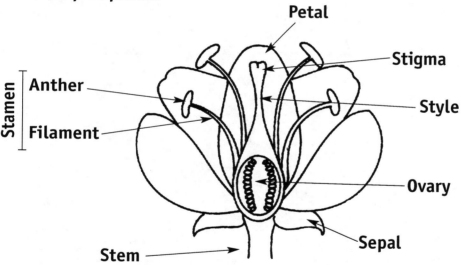

Procedure

1. Find the different parts of your flower.

2. Take the petals off the flower.

3. Take out the stamen. Gently wipe it on the black paper.

4. Use the toothpick to open the ovary.

Experiment: The Parts of a Flower (cont'd.)

5. Look at all the parts with the magnifying glass.

6. Have an adult slice the apple in half from top to bottom.

7. Compare the apple to the lily.

Analysis

1. What did you see when you rubbed the stamen on the black paper?

_____

_____

_____

2. What did the inside of the apple look like?

_____

_____

_____

Conclusion

What part of the lily is the apple most like?

_____

_____

_____

Lesson 6 Organisms and Environments

You wouldn't expect to walk down the street and run into a penguin. Penguins live in very specific environments. They live where the temperatures are cold and where they can find the food they need. Every organism lives in an environment that provides the things it needs to survive.

The environment in which an organism lives is known as its ecosystem. An **ecosystem** is made up of the living and the nonliving things in an environment. A fish tank, for example, can be considered a small ecosystem. It is made up of the fish and plants in the tank. The water, rocks, and filter are also parts of the ecosystem.

An ecosystem can be thought of as organisms living together and interacting with each other and the environment.

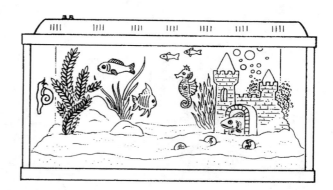

Populations

There are millions of different types of organisms on Earth. Each type of organism is known as a species. More specifically, a

Key Terms

ecosystem—the living and nonliving things in an environment

species—a group of similar organisms that can reproduce

population—all of the organisms of the same species living in one area

community—all of the populations of organisms living in the same place

producer—an organism that can make food

consumer—an organism that must eat other living things to get energy

food chain—the flow of energy from producers to consumers in an ecosystem

decomposer—an organism that breaks down wastes or bodies of dead organisms

food web—the overlapping food chains in an ecosystem

energy pyramid—a diagram that shows that the amount of available energy decreases along a food chain

species is a group of similar organisms that can reproduce. The young, or offspring, that are produced can grow up to reproduce as well. For example, lions, tigers, and panthers are animals. They are all types of cats. However, each type of cat is a different species.

A group of organisms of the same species living in the same area makes up a **population**. All of the alligators living in a swamp form a population. An ecosystem may have many different populations of organisms. The same swamp that has a population of alligators may also have a population of egrets. The egrets might make up only one of the many bird populations in the swamp. In the same way, a population of mangrove trees might be only one of the plant populations in the swamp.

Communities

All of the populations that live in the same area make up a **community**. This means that the alligators, birds, trees, and other populations in a swamp form a community. Organisms in a community interact. This means that they affect one another. Plants supply animals with energy. Plants might also provide homes for animals. Plants depend on animals to produce oxygen. Some plants also depend on animals to carry their seeds and other materials away.

Roles of Organisms

Every organism plays an important role in its ecosystem. Scientists name general groups of organisms according to their role. Plants and other organisms that conduct photosynthesis are known as **producers**. These organisms use the energy of sunlight to *produce* food. All of the organisms in the ecosystem depend on the food that producers make. They use the energy stored in this food for all the processes they need to survive.

Organisms that eat other living things for energy are called **consumers**. A consumer, such as a mouse, might feed directly on a producer. A consumer might also feed on an organism that has eaten a producer. For example, an owl might eat a gopher that has eaten grass. The flow of energy from producers to consumers is called a **food chain**.

You might think that the materials and energy in an organism's body are lost to an ecosystem once the organism dies. This is not the case. Organisms known as **decomposers** break down wastes or bodies of dead organisms. In the process, they return the materials to the ecosystem. Fungi, such as mushrooms, and bacteria act as decomposers in many ecosystems.

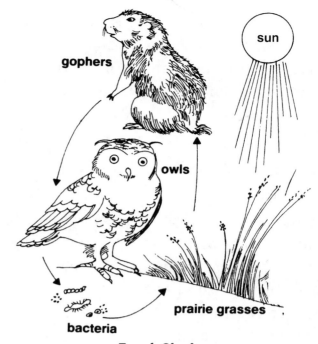

Food Chain

Food Webs

In any ecosystem, several different food chains might overlap. This means that the same plant might be the producer for

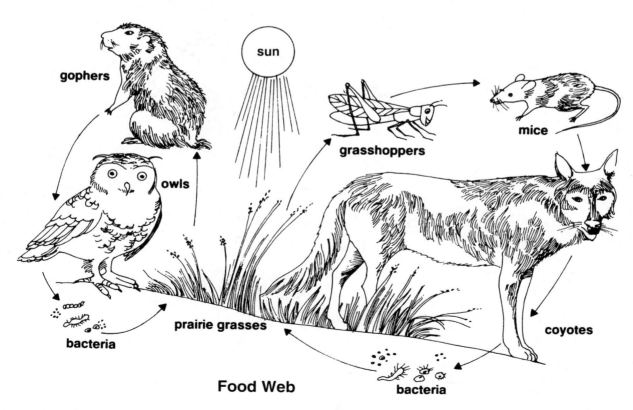

Food Web

more than one food chain. It might also mean that a consumer might feed on organisms from different food chains. A **food web** shows how different food chains are related.

Energy Pyramid

The number of organisms in each population in an ecosystem can be very different. In a particular ecosystem, there may be many plants, but only a few wolves. The reason has to do with how energy flows through the ecosystem. Remember that producers use the energy of sunlight to produce food. Food contains stored energy. Producers use some of the energy and store the rest.

When a consumer feeds on a plant, it gets some of the stored energy. The remaining stored energy is changed into heat that is transferred to the environment. Therefore, only a small portion of the producer's energy is passed along to the consumer. Only 10 percent of the energy of the plant is passed along to the consumer that eats it.

A diagram called an **energy pyramid** shows how energy is passed along a food chain. The wide base shows that the lowest level of the food chain has the greatest amount of energy. The narrow point at the top shows that the amount of available energy decreases as you move along the food chain. The energy pyramid can help you see why an ecosystem has more producers than large consumers. There is not enough energy available to support large populations of consumers.

Lesson 6

Review

Darken the circle by the best answer.

1. All of the living and nonliving things in an environment make up
   - (A) an ecosystem.
   - (B) a population.
   - (C) a community.
   - (D) a food chain.

2. Which of the following is an example of a species?
   - (A) all of the animals in a zoo
   - (B) all of the plants in a rain forest
   - (C) all of the dogs at a dog show
   - (D) all of the fish in a lake

3. All of the white-tailed deer in a forest make up
   - (A) an ecosystem.
   - (B) a population.
   - (C) a community.
   - (D) a food chain.

4. Which of these organisms is a producer in its ecosystem?
   - (A) frog
   - (B) grass
   - (C) snake
   - (D) owl

5. The organisms in an ecosystem have jobs much like people in a community. What is the job of a decomposer?
   - (A) to deliver something
   - (B) to fix something
   - (C) to make a product
   - (D) to recycle materials

6. Which shape can be used to represent the flow of energy through an ecosystem?
   - (A) ball
   - (B) box
   - (C) pyramid
   - (D) stairs

7. In what way do animals depend on plants in an ecosystem?

   food

   _____

   _____

8. Why does the amount of available energy decrease along a food chain?

   it gets used up

   _____

   _____

Lesson 6   A Frozen Food Chain

Below are pictures of organisms that live in an arctic, or very cold, environment. Write the name of each organism in the food chain.

[Hint: Pay attention to the sizes of the organisms to help you decide where to place them. Some organisms are eaten by more than one other organism.]

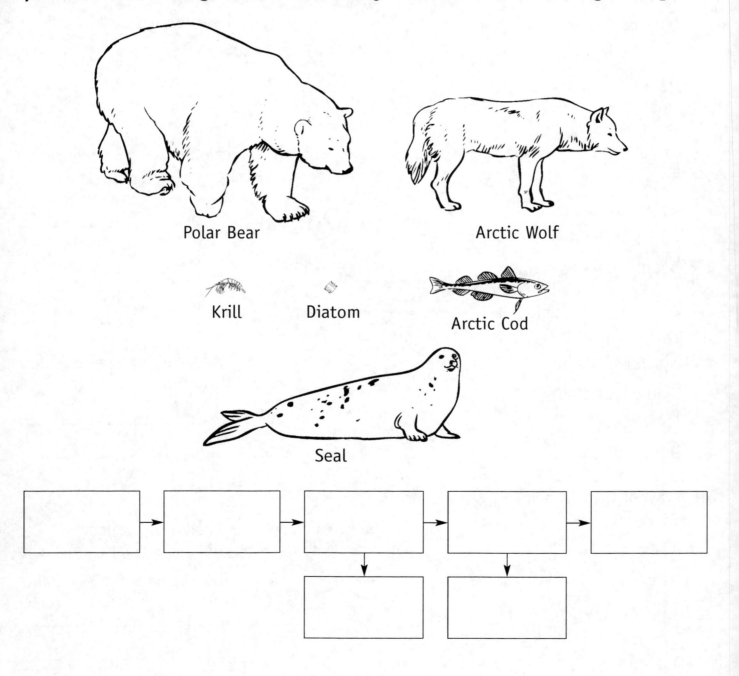

Polar Bear   Arctic Wolf

Krill   Diatom   Arctic Cod

Seal

Lesson 6

Making Predictions

The diagram below shows a food web for an ecosystem. Study the diagram and then answer the questions that follow.

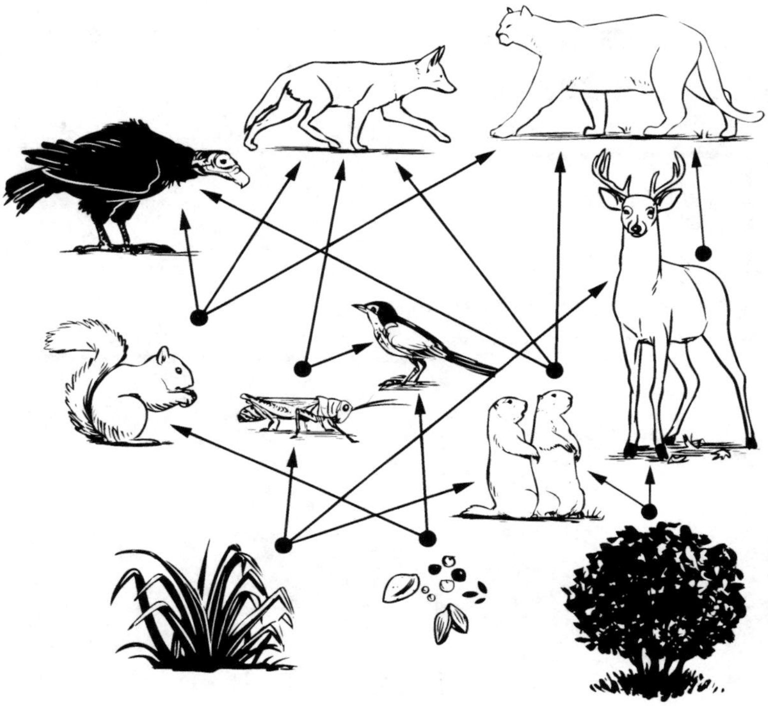

1. Which organisms depend on grasshoppers for food?

fox, bird

2. Suppose the deer are removed from the ecosystem. What will happen to the population of mountain lions if the deer population decreases?

death

3. Suppose a chemical spills into the ecosystem and kills much of the grass. Which organisms will be most directly affected by the loss of the grass?

grass hoppers
merekats

Lesson 6   Describing Organisms

Circle the following words in the puzzle below. They may appear horizontally, vertically, or diagonally.

After you find all of the words, circle the letters that are not used. The first few letters will reveal a hidden message. Write the message on the lines below the puzzle.

COMMUNITY   CONSUMER   DECOMPOSER   FOOD CHAIN

FOOD WEB   POPULATION   PRODUCER   SPECIES

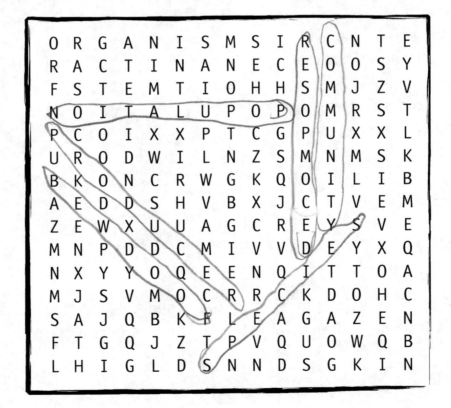

_____

_____

_____

Lesson 6

Biomes of the World

Read the following passage and review the chart. Then answer the questions that follow.

What is it like where you live? What kinds of plants and animals live there? Scientists divide Earth into regions called biomes. A biome is an environment made up of similar ecosystems. It is described by the organisms that live in it as well as the type of soil and the general climate. The climate of a place is the type of weather it has over a long period of time. The chart below lists some of Earth's major biomes. It also gives a few of the major plants and animals that live in the biome.

Biome	Climate	Animals	Plants
Tundra	This biome can be found in very cold places. It has long cold winters and little rain or snow.	arctic foxes, musk oxen, arctic hares	Only small plants such as mosses and dwarfed shrubs grow here.
Taiga	This biome is a little warmer and wetter than the tundra, but still cold through most of the year.	lynxes, elks, moose, and beavers	Spruce, fir, and pine trees are the main plants.
Temperate Forest	This biome has trees that change colors in the fall. This biome has four seasons and rain is spread evenly throughout the year.	white-tail deer, gray squirrels, chipmunks, raccoons, opossums, skunks, wolves, mountain lions, and bobcats	Oak, beech, and chestnut trees are common.
Tropical Forest	This biome is known for warm temperatures and plenty of rain all year long.	monkeys, snakes, toucans	Thick layers of trees, vines, shrubs, and ferns fill this biome.
Desert	This biome gets very little rain. Temperatures can vary from very hot to very cold. The soil is sandy.	snakes, lizards, camels, foxes	Cactuses and shrubs are the main plants.

Biomes of the World (cont'd.)

1. Which description best describes a climate?

   Ⓐ high and steep

   Ⓑ long and thin

   Ⓒ warm and rainy

   Ⓓ dark and brown

2. The saguaro is a plant that thrives in hot conditions with very little water. It is found in only one biome on Earth. In which biome is the saguaro most likely found?

   Ⓐ tundra

   Ⓑ tropical forest

   Ⓒ taiga

   Ⓓ desert

3. Some animals from the tundra travel to slightly warmer temperatures in winter. Which biome is just a little warmer than the tundra and has many tall trees?

   Ⓐ taiga

   Ⓑ temperate forest

   Ⓒ tropical forest

   Ⓓ desert

4. One of the biomes is like a desert because it gets very little rain. Its temperatures, however, are very different. This biome is the

   Ⓐ taiga.

   Ⓑ tundra.

   Ⓒ temperate forest.

   Ⓓ tropical forest.

Lesson 6   Experiment: Insect Habitats

The habitat of an insect can be small. Different types of insects can live in different parts of the same yard. In this activity, you will find out which insects live in habitats of your yard.

What You Will Need

clear, plastic container
sweet food such as jelly, honey, or fruit
magnifying glass

Procedure

1. Dig a small hole in your yard at home or at school.

2. Place a clean, plastic container in the hole. The rim of the container should be even with the ground.

3. Add bait to the container. Use jelly, honey, or small pieces of fruit.

4. Leave the area for at least 30 minutes.

5. Go back and observe the container. See if any insects are in it. Look at them with a magnifying glass. Draw pictures of them and write down what you see.

6. Set the insects free. Repeat Steps 1 through 5 in a different part of the yard.

Analysis

What types of insects did you see?

_____

_____

Conclusion

Did different insects live in different habitats? Explain.

_____

_____

Lesson 7 Properties of Earth Materials

When you walk on a white, sandy beach, you are probably enjoying one of Earth's many minerals—quartz. **Minerals** have five basic properties.

1. A mineral is a solid. A solid object is one that has a definite shape and volume.

2. A mineral occurs naturally on Earth. This means that it must be formed by processes that happen in nature.

3. A mineral is inorganic. This term means that a mineral is not made from materials that were once part of living things.

4. A mineral has a crystal structure. A crystal is made up of particles that line up in a pattern. This causes crystals to have flat sides with sharp edges.

5. A mineral always contains specific substances that are present in a certain ratio. A ratio compares two amounts.

Key Terms

mineral—a solid, naturally occurring, inorganic crystal structure that has a definite chemical makeup

streak—the color of the powder left behind when a mineral is rubbed across a tile surface

cleavage—a property of minerals that split along flat surfaces

fracture—a property of minerals that break apart unevenly

weathering—the process through which natural forces, such as wind and water, break down rocks and other materials into small pieces

sediment—a small piece of solid material that has been broken down by weathering

erosion—the process through which natural forces, such as wind and water, carry away bits of rock and other materials over time

deposition—the process through which sediments are dropped in one place

sedimentary rock—a type of rock formed when layers of sediment become squeezed and glued together by natural processes

igneous rock—a type of rock formed from the cooling of lava or magma

metamorphic rock—a type of rock formed when high heat and pressure change one form of rock into another

For example, the mineral quartz has one atom of an element called silicon for every atom of oxygen.

Properties of Minerals

Scientists who study minerals and related materials are known as geologists. By looking carefully at the characteristics of substances, geologists have discovered about 3,800 different minerals. Each one can be described by its properties.

Color The color of a mineral can be seen by simply looking at it. While color is an important property of minerals, it is not enough to identify a sample. This is because several different minerals may all have the same color. The mineral pyrite is known as "fool's gold" because it has the same color as real gold.

Luster The luster of a mineral describes how shiny it is. A mineral that has a high luster reflects light that is shined on it.

Streak If you rub a mineral across a tile surface, it will leave a powder behind. The color of the powder is the mineral's **streak**. The streak of a mineral is important because samples of the same mineral can have slightly different colors. The streak, however, is always the same for any given mineral.

Hardness Minerals can be described by how hard they are. Diamond, for example, is the hardest known mineral. In 1812, a mineral expert named Friedrich Mohs developed a scale to compare the hardness of minerals. The scale, now known as

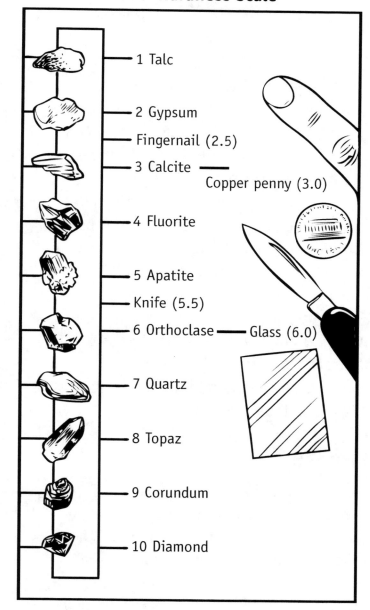

Mohs' Hardness Scale

1 Talc
2 Gypsum
Fingernail (2.5)
3 Calcite
Copper penny (3.0)
4 Fluorite
5 Apatite
Knife (5.5)
6 Orthoclase — Glass (6.0)
7 Quartz
8 Topaz
9 Corundum
10 Diamond

Mohs' hardness scale, places ten minerals in order from softest (1) to hardest (10).

A mineral can scratch any softer mineral. It can be scratched by minerals that are harder. Geologists can use a scratch test to determine hardness. Suppose that a sample can scratch calcite but not fluorite. This means that its

Lesson 7, Properties of Earth Materials
Science 4, SV 9781419034329

hardness must be between these two minerals on the scale. Its hardness must be between 3 and 4.

Cleavage and Fracture Geologists look at the way that a mineral breaks apart. A mineral that splits along flat surfaces has a property called **cleavage**. If a mineral breaks apart unevenly instead, it is said to have **fracture**.

Special Properties Some minerals have other properties that can be used to identify them. Some minerals act like magnets. Magnetite is a naturally magnetic mineral. Others, such as scheelite, glow when they are placed under a certain type of light known as ultraviolet light. Still other minerals, such as calcite, bend light when it passes through them.

Rocks

Rocks are solid objects made up of minerals and other materials. In some rocks, there is only one mineral. Other rocks contain a few different minerals. Granite, for example, contains at least four different minerals—quartz, feldspar, hornblende, and mica.

Geologists divide rocks into three major groups depending on how they were formed. These groups are sedimentary rock, igneous rock, and metamorphic rock.

Sedimentary Rock Over time, wind, water, and other natural forces break pieces off of rocks. This process is known as **weathering**. The small, solid pieces of material that come from rocks, or even living things, make up **sediment**. The same process that caused weathering can carry sediment to a new location. This process is known as **erosion**.

When sediments are dropped in the same place over time, they build up in layers. This process is known as **deposition**. As the layers of sediment grow, the heavy layers at the top push down on the layers below them. This causes the sediments to be tightly squeezed together. In addition, chemical changes cause the sediments to become glued together. The result is **sedimentary rock**.

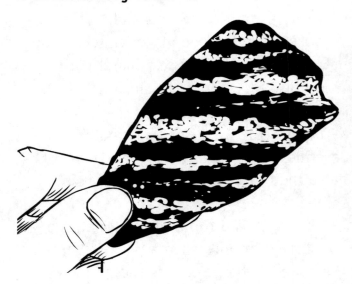

Igneous Rock Perhaps you have seen pictures of lava flowing from a volcano. Lava is rock that is so hot it has melted. When lava cools down, it forms solid rock known as **igneous rock**. Some igneous rocks form on Earth's surface. Other igneous rocks form from magma below Earth's surface. Magma is like lava. However, lava is on top of Earth's surface and magma is below it.

Metamorphic Rock When you push down on something, you apply pressure to it. Below Earth's surface, rocks experience tremendous pressure. They can also experience great heat. Pressure and heat below Earth's surface can change other rocks into **metamorphic rock**.

The Rock Cycle

The processes that occur on Earth constantly change the form and structure of rocks. These changes can be described by a series of processes known as the rock cycle.

Use your finger to trace some of the pathways represented by the arrows in the diagram of the rock cycle. For example, magma cools and hardens into igneous rock. Over time, weathering might break down the igneous rock into sediments. Through erosion and deposition, the sediments pile up in layers to form sedimentary rock. Weathering and erosion might break that rock down again. Or high heat and pressure might cause it to change into metamorphic rock. Conditions below Earth's surface might cause the rock to melt into magma or lava. This starts the cycle again. Look for other paths in the diagram.

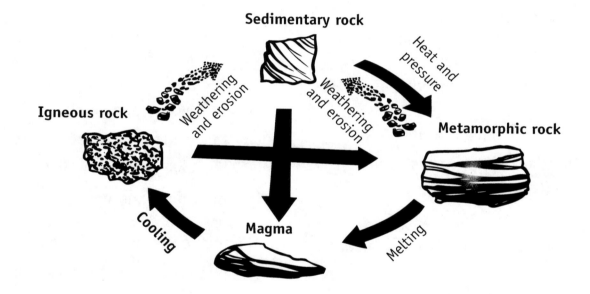

Lesson 7   Review

Darken the circle by the best answer.

1. Which of these is NOT necessarily a property of all minerals?

    (A) They must be solids.

    (B) They must occur naturally on Earth.

    (C) They must be worth a lot of money.

    (D) They must not come from materials of living organisms.

2. Which of these does a geologist do to check for a mineral's streak?

    (A) Break the mineral in half.

    (B) Rub the mineral across a tile surface.

    (C) Soak the mineral in water.

    (D) Scratch the mineral with diamond.

3. The process through which natural forces break rocks into small pieces is known as

    (A) deposition.

    (B) refraction.

    (C) melting.

    (D) weathering.

4. How is magma different from lava?

    (A) Lava comes from earthquakes, but magma comes from volcanoes.

    (B) Lava is hot, but magma is cool.

    (C) Lava is above the ground, but magma is under the ground.

    (D) Lava forms in water, but magma forms in soil.

5. What conditions lead to the making of metamorphic rock?

    (A) cold water and wind

    (B) tall mountains and heavy rain

    (C) hot lava and steep hills

    (D) high heat and pressure

6. The rock cycle describes how

    (A) one type of rock changes into another.

    (B) rocks move over Earth's surface.

    (C) rocks block the path of moving water.

    (D) rocks form in round shapes.

7. A scientist develops a fake diamond in the laboratory. It looks just like a real diamond. Why can't it be considered a mineral?

_____

_____

_____

8. How might igneous rock change into sedimentary rock?

_____

_____

_____

_____

_____

Lesson 7   Earth's Materials

Write a key term to complete each sentence. Choose from the words below.

cleavage	metamorphic	deposition	minerals
erosion	sedimentary	igneous	streak

1. A(n) _____ rock is formed when lava from a volcano cools down.

2. The process of _____ carries away small pieces of sediment.

3. A mineral with _____ splits along flat surfaces.

4. Gold and quartz are examples of _____.

5. _____ rock is formed when bits of rock and other matter pile up over time.

6. Any type of rock can change into _____ rock due to high heat and pressure.

7. As a result of _____, sediment is dropped in a location over time.

8. A mineral's _____ is the color of the powder left behind when it is rubbed across a tile surface.

Lesson 7

Properties of Minerals and Rocks

Complete the puzzle with the terms described by each clue on the next page. Choose from the word bank below.

| deposition | erosion | fracture | hardness | igneous rock | luster |
| magnetite | metamorphic rock | mineral | rock | rock cycle | streak |

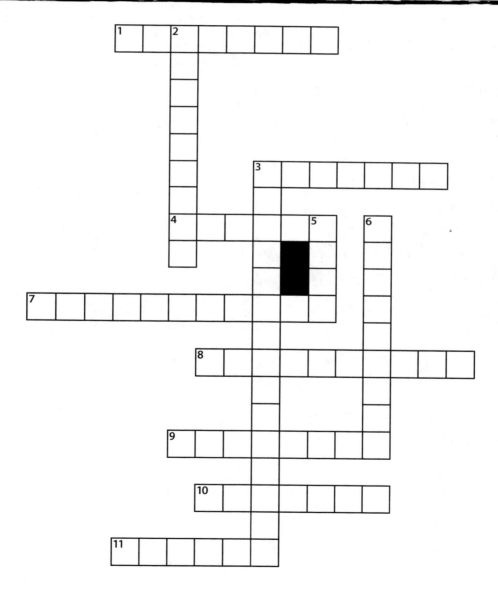

Properties of Minerals and Rocks (cont'd.)

Across

1. a property of minerals that tells which mineral will scratch another

3. a naturally occurring inorganic solid with a crystal structure

4. a mineral property that tells how well the mineral reflects light

7. the type of rock formed from volcanic lava

8. the piling up of sediment carried by erosion

9. the property of minerals that break apart unevenly

10. the process through which a weathered rock is carried away by wind or water over time

11. the colored powder left behind when a mineral is rubbed across a tile surface

Down

2. the continuous process through which rocks change into other types of rocks

3. the type of rock formed when other types of rocks are exposed to high heat and pressure

5. a solid material made up of minerals and other substances

6. a mineral that has magnetic properties

Lesson 7

The Grand Canyon

Read the following passage. Then answer the questions that follow the passage.

In one of America's oldest national parks, the Grand Canyon is a magnificent sight. Located in Arizona, the Grand Canyon is more than 400 kilometers long and more than a kilometer deep. In some places, it is more than 30 kilometers wide.

This wonderful attraction was not carved out by people. Instead, it was formed by the continuous motion of the Colorado River. The moving water has been wearing away the rock and soil below for millions of years. The sediments are then carried away by the moving water. They are eventually deposited in other locations.

In addition to the weathering and erosion by the river, other natural forces carve away at the sides of the canyon. Wind, for example, blows away rock and soil from the sides. Rain water carries away more sediment. Even mud sliding down the walls of the canyon causes erosion. Each day, about one-half million tons of sediment are carried out of the canyon.

1. Where is the Grand Canyon located?

(A) Colorado

(B) California

(C) Washington

(D) Arizona

2. What is the main factor in forming the Grand Canyon?

(A) moving water

(B) digging trucks

(C) running animals

(D) flowing lava

3. What happens to the sediment formed by erosion in the canyon?

(A) It piles up to make the canyon smaller.

(B) It adds to the sides to make the canyon more narrow.

(C) It is carried away by wind and water.

(D) It is changed into sedimentary rock at the bottom of the river.

4. What will most likely happen to the Grand Canyon over the next thousand years?

(A) It will gradually become flat land.

(B) It will continue to grow deeper.

(C) It will fill up with water and become a lake.

(D) It will fill in with sediment and become solid rock.

Lesson 7   Experiment: Investigating Weathering

Weathering happens to the surface of rocks. The surface area of a rock is the amount of the rock that is exposed to natural forces. How does the rate of weathering change if a rock is broken into smaller rocks? In this experiment you will use sugar samples to model rock samples in order to answer this question.

What You Will Need

sugar cube
teaspoon of granulated sugar
two identical small containers
water
2 stirrers (or spoons)
stopwatch

Procedure

1. Fill each container halfway with water.
2. Add the sugar cube to one container.
3. Add a teaspoon of granulated sugar to the other container.
4. Stir the sugar in each container with different stirrers. Be sure to stir both containers for the same amount of time.
5. Measure the time it takes for the sugar to dissolve in each container. Record your measurements.

Analysis

Sample	Time
Container 1 (sugar cube)	
Container 2 (granulated sugar)	

Experiment: Investigating Weathering (cont'd.)

1. Why did you need to use the same amount of sugar and water in each container?

_____

_____

_____

2. What difference was provided by using granulated sugar and a sugar cube?

_____

_____

_____

3. Which sugar sample dissolved first?

_____

_____

_____

Conclusion

How is the rate of weathering affected by breaking rock into smaller rocks?

_____

_____

_____

Lesson 8 Objects in the Sky

What do you see when you look up into the sky? Perhaps you see the sun or the moon. Maybe you see planets and stars. Many of these objects are part of our solar system. A **solar system** is a group of objects in space that move around a star. The path an object follows as it moves around another object is known as an **orbit**.

The central star in our solar system is the sun. Like other stars, the sun is a ball of burning gases. It is hard to imagine just how large the sun is. It is more than 1 million kilometers across! Next to the sun, even Earth looks small.

The Planets

Earth is one of the planets that move around the sun. A **planet** is a large object that moves around a star. The other

Mercury   Venus   Earth   Mars   Jupiter   Saturn   Uranus   Neptune

Key Terms

solar system—a group of objects in space that move around a star

orbit—the path an object follows as it travels around another object in space

planet—a large object that moves around a star

satellite—an object that orbits a larger object in space

asteroid—a small rocky object in space

comet—a small mass of ice and dust that orbits the sun in a long path

meteor—a piece of rock or dust that glows when entering Earth's atmosphere

meteoroid—a piece of rock or dust before it enters Earth's atmosphere

meteorite—the remains of a meteor that reaches Earth's surface

star—a glowing ball of gas

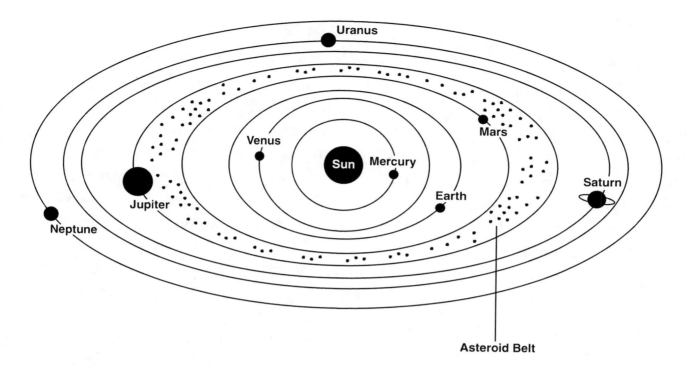

Asteroid Belt

planets in this solar system include Mercury, Venus, Mars, Jupiter, Saturn, Uranus, and Neptune. Some planets, such as Earth, are hard and made up of rock. Other planets, such as Neptune, are made up mostly of gases.

Many of the planets have at least one moon. A moon is an object that moves around a planet. A moon can be described as a natural **satellite**. Earth has just one moon. Some planets, such as Jupiter and Saturn, have many moons. Other planets, such as Mercury, do not have any moons.

Asteroids, Comets, and Meteors

A number of small rocky objects known as **asteroids** also travel around the sun. Although they have been found throughout the solar system, most of them

are in a cluster between Mars and Jupiter. This cluster is known as the Asteroid Belt.

Hundreds of thousands of asteroids have been discovered. If the masses of all these asteroids were added together, the total would be less than the mass of Earth's moon. Asteroids are known as minor planets because they are made of the same materials as planets. However, they are much smaller.

Although many objects in the solar system were not discovered until the telescope was invented, comets were seen long before. A **comet** is a small mass of dust and ice that travels around the sun in a long path. Comets cannot be seen until they get close to the sun. When this happens, some of the ice in the comet changes into water vapor. It streams out from the central part of the comet, forming a long, glowing tail. This is what can be seen from Earth.

Many comets have large paths, or orbits, that take them to the edges of the solar system. They are seen once and then disappear for thousands of years. Some comets, however, have shorter orbits. Scientists have been able to track their paths and predict when they can be seen again. Perhaps the most famous comet is Halley's comet. It can be seen about every 76 years. This comet was last seen in 1986 and is predicted to return in 2062.

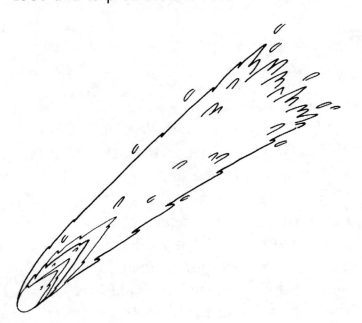

If you have ever seen a shooting star in the nighttime sky, you have witnessed a meteor. A **meteor** is a piece of dust or rock that glows as it enters Earth's atmosphere. Before reaching Earth's atmosphere, it is known as a **meteoroid**. Most of a meteor burns up as it travels through Earth's atmosphere. If any remains to reach the ground, it is called a **meteorite**. On any given night, several meteors can be seen. On some nights, though, hundreds of meteors can be seen in what is known as a meteor shower.

Stars

The sun is just one of many stars in the universe. A **star** is a glowing ball of gas. The heat and light from a star are produced by nuclear reactions within the star. During a nuclear reaction, particles of matter change into other particles. In the process, they give off huge amounts of energy as heat and light.

The sun is average in size when compared to other stars. There are many smaller stars, but there are many larger stars as well. The reason that the sun looks so large to people on Earth is because the sun is closer to Earth than any other star is.

Though they are not living organisms, stars go through a life cycle. Stars are born when huge clouds of dust and gas are pulled tightly together. A star might remain the same for millions of years. As the star gets old, however, it begins to run out of the gases needed for its nuclear reactions. The star begins to cool down, and it becomes larger. In this stage, the star is known as a red giant. The sun is expected to reach this stage in about 5 billion years.

If the original mass of the star was relatively small, the outer layers of the star will come apart. The hot, dense center that is left behind will form what is known as a white dwarf. A white dwarf does not have any more fuel to burn. It glows only because of its leftover heat. Over billions of years, it will eventually fade out.

If the original mass of the star was great, the star will become a very large red giant. For these stars, this stage is known as a red supergiant. These stars then experience a huge explosion known as a supernova. Materials from the star are sent out into space. Anything that remains from the core of the star can form a different kind of star called a neutron star. It can also form what is known as a black hole. A black hole is named so because it pulls anything near it inside—even light.

Life Cycle of a Massive Star

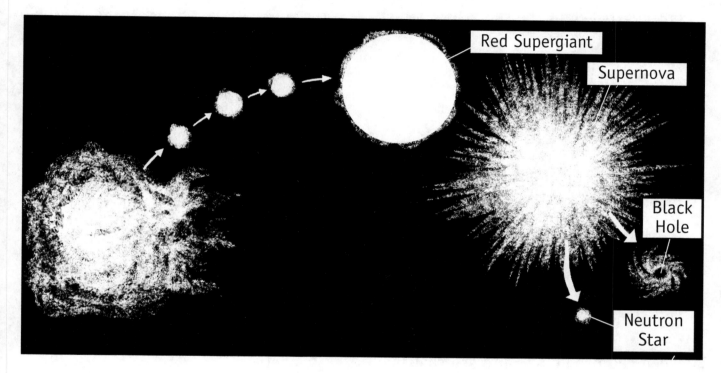

Lesson 8   **Review**

Darken the circle by the best answer.

1. The sun, the planets, and the other objects that orbit the sun make up the
   - (A) solar system.
   - (B) sky.
   - (C) universe.
   - (D) satellites.

2. Between Mars and Jupiter can be found a large cluster of
   - (A) meteors.
   - (B) comets.
   - (C) asteroids.
   - (D) planets.

3. When can people on Earth see comets?
   - (A) when comets turn into stars
   - (B) when comets explode
   - (C) when comets come close to Earth
   - (D) when comets move near the sun

4. Another name for a shooting star is a
   - (A) meteoroid.
   - (B) meteor.
   - (C) meteorite.
   - (D) meter.

5. What makes the heat and light from the sun and other stars?
   - (A) chemical changes
   - (B) electricity
   - (C) nuclear reactions
   - (D) lightning storms

6. What happens during a supernova?
   - (A) A white dwarf fades out.
   - (B) A black hole absorbs light.
   - (C) A star is born.
   - (D) A supergiant star explodes.

7. Why isn't the moon considered to be a planet?

   _____

   _____

8. For thousands of years, people have written down when they saw comets. Why are some comets seen only once, but others are seen more than once?

   _____

   _____

9. Describe the life cycle of the sun.

   _____

   _____

Lesson 8   **Shooting Stars**

The diagram shows a meteor, meteoroid, and meteorite. Label each one on the lines provided. Then write a sentence or two describing each one. Tell how they are alike and how they are different.

1. _____

2. _____

3. _____

_____

_____

_____

_____

Lesson 8, Shooting Stars
Science 4, SV 9781419034329

Lesson 8

Describing Objects in the Sky

Unscramble each of the clue words.

Unscramble the letters that appear in boxes to find the final message.

1. TOBIR

2. LITLAETES

3. REISODTA

4. PTLEAN

5. TECOM

6. ROEMET

7. RATS

8. ☐☐☐☐☐ ☐Y☐☐☐☐

www.harcourtschoolsupply.com
© Harcourt Achieve Inc. All rights reserved.

98

Lesson 8, Describing Objects in the Sky
Science 4, SV 9781419034329

Lesson 8   Supernovas

Read the following passage. Then answer the questions that follow the passage.

Imagine learning about history by looking into the sky. That's just what happens if you see a supernova. A supernova marks the end of a star's lifetime. When a star explodes, it becomes the brightest object in the sky. A supernova may last for a day, a week, or even longer.

People who study stars are known as astronomers. Throughout history, astronomers have seen many supernovas. Many of the exploding stars are very far from Earth. Often, by the time the light from the explosion travels all the way to Earth, the supernova has already ended. Even so, the date described for each supernova is the year during which it was seen. When a supernova is seen, it is named by the year in which it is observed. The year is followed by a letter telling the order in which it was seen. For example, the first supernova seen in 1987 was named SN 1987A. The SN stands for supernova.

Supernovas in faraway galaxies are common to see. A galaxy is a large group of stars. Our solar system is in a galaxy known as the Milky Way Galaxy. Supernovas in this galaxy are less common. The last supernova seen in this galaxy was seen in 1604. It was identified by the famous astronomer Johannes Kepler.

Astronomers use information about supernovas to learn about the universe. One question astronomers try to answer has to do with whether or not the universe is getting larger. Astronomers know how fast light travels. They can then use light from supernovas to figure out how far away another galaxy is. If that distance is longer than it was during an earlier supernova, they can conclude that the galaxy is moving away.

1. Why might a supernova explosion be over by the time it is seen from Earth?

_____

_____

2. What would be the name of the fourth supernova seen in the year 2010?

_____

3. How can an astronomer use a supernova to decide if the universe is getting larger?

_____

_____

Lesson 8   Experiment: Investigating Star Brightness

To people on Earth, the sun appears to be the brightest star in the sky. If you compare it to other stars in the universe, the sun is not the brightest or the largest. What determines how bright a star looks from Earth? Try this experiment to find out.

What You Will Need

2 identical flashlights

Procedure

1. Dim the lights in a classroom or hallway.
2. Put two identical flashlights next to each other on a flat surface. Then turn both flashlights on.
3. Without looking directly into the flashlights, compare how bright they appear. Write down your observations.
4. Move one of the flashlights closer to you. Repeat Step 3.
5. Move the flashlight that is farther away even farther away. Repeat Step 3.

Analysis

1. Which flashlight looked brighter after you moved them to different distances?

_____

_____

2. Suppose you were able to replace one of the flashlights with one that is brighter than the other. How could you make both flashlights appear to have the same brightness?

_____

_____

Conclusion

How might a star that is brighter than the sun look as if it is not as bright?

_____

_____

Lesson 9 Changes in Earth and Sky

Each day you wake to a new morning. The darkness of night is broken by the rising sun. At night, the sun sets again and the cycle repeats. What causes the continuous change between day and night? It is the motion of Earth.

Day and Night

Have you ever spun a top? If so, you know that it spins in a circle. In a similar way, Earth spins around an imaginary line known as the **axis**. The axis runs through the center of Earth from the North Pole to the South Pole. The spinning motion is called **rotation**. Earth completes one rotation every 24 hours, or one day.

As Earth rotates, the part of Earth facing the sun changes. The part of Earth facing the sun is lit up and has daytime. The part of Earth facing away from the sun is in darkness and has nighttime. In this way, the rotation of Earth causes day and night.

Seasons

While Earth is rotating on its axis, it is traveling around the sun in an orbit. The movement around the sun is called its **revolution**. Earth completes one revolution in about 365 days, or one year.

Earth's axis is slightly tilted. This means that for almost half of the year, the Northern Hemisphere points toward the sun. At the same time, the Southern Hemisphere points away from the sun. The Northern Hemisphere is the top half of Earth. The Southern Hemisphere is the bottom half of Earth.

Key Terms

axis—an imaginary line that runs from the North Pole to the South Pole of Earth

rotation—the spinning on an axis

revolution—the movement of Earth around the sun

phases of the moon—the changes in the appearance of the moon because of its motion around Earth

constellation—a group of stars that has been given a name according to an imaginary picture it forms

When the Northern Hemisphere points toward the sun, it receives more direct energy from sunlight. This causes it to have longer days and higher temperatures. The Northern Hemisphere experiences summer. At the same time, the Southern Hemisphere receives less direct sunlight. As a result, it has shorter days and colder temperatures. The Southern Hemisphere experiences winter.

Six months later, the conditions are opposite. The Northern Hemisphere points away from the sun and has winter. At the same time, the Southern Hemisphere points toward the sun and has summer.

At two points in Earth's orbit, neither hemisphere points toward or away from the sun. These two points mark the beginning of spring and fall.

Phases of the Moon

If you look at the moon tonight, it will look different than it did two weeks ago. It might look like a circle, half of a circle, or even a curve. The moon doesn't actually change shape. Instead, the moon's appearance, or how it looks, changes.

The moon does not make its own light. It is lit up by the sun. As on Earth, half of the moon faces the sun and is lit. The other half faces away from the sun and is dark.

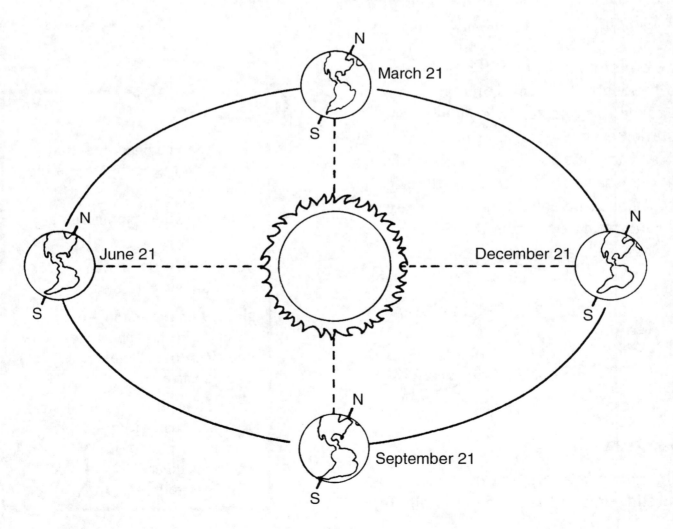

www.harcourtschoolsupply.com
102
Lesson 9, Changes in Earth and Sky
Science 4, SV 9781419034329

The Moon's Eight Phases

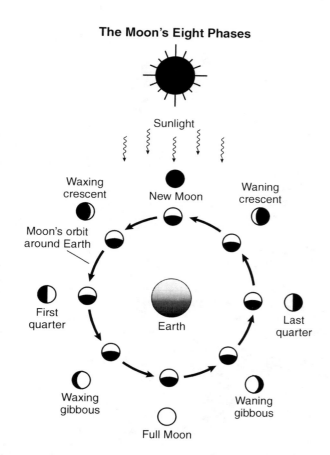

The moon orbits Earth much like Earth orbits the sun. It takes about 28 days for the moon to orbit Earth. As the moon orbits Earth, different amounts of the lit half can be seen from Earth. The different shapes of the moon are known as the **phases of the moon**.

Look at the moon in the diagram at the top of the page. Find the place when the moon is between Earth and the sun. During this phase, known as the new moon, a person on Earth can't see any of the lit half of the moon. Now find the place when Earth is between the moon and the sun. During this phase, known as the full moon, a person on Earth can see all of the lit half of the moon.

Trace the moon as it moves from the new moon phase to the full moon phase. You can see that more and more of the lit half can be seen from Earth. After the full moon phase, less and less of the lit half can be seen from Earth. Then the cycle of phases begins again.

Constellations

For thousands of years, people have been studying the stars in the sky. Long ago, people noticed that many stars exist in groups. Much like playing a game of connect-the-dots, people imagined pictures formed by the stars. A **constellation** is a group of stars that has been given a name relating to the picture it forms.

There are 88 constellations. Examples of constellations include a bear, a lion, and a hunter. Scientists who study stars, called astronomers, divide the sky into sections by these constellations.

If you study constellations, you will find that the constellations you can see in December are different from those you can see in June. The reason is that as Earth orbits the sun, its view of the universe changes. Before calendars were developed, people used the constellations to predict the seasons. This was especially important to people who needed to know when to plant crops. The diagram provides examples of some of the constellations as they might be seen by a person in a specific location at a certain time.

CONSTELLATIONS

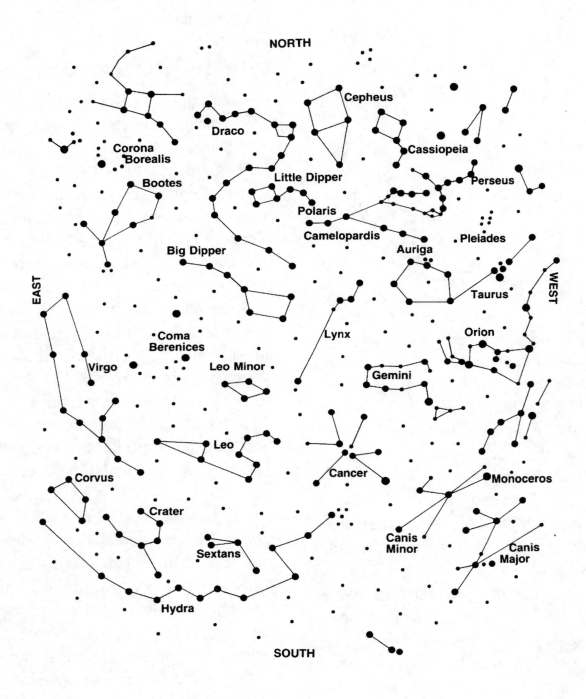

Lesson 9

Review

Darken the circle by the best answer.

1. Which length of time is determined by one rotation on Earth?

   Ⓐ minute

   Ⓑ hour

   Ⓒ day

   Ⓓ year

2. If Earth took longer to complete one revolution,

   Ⓐ night would last longer.

   Ⓑ day would last longer.

   Ⓒ the moon would not change phases as quickly.

   Ⓓ a year would last longer.

3. The Northern Hemisphere has summer when

   Ⓐ it is closest to the sun.

   Ⓑ it points toward the sun.

   Ⓒ it points toward the moon.

   Ⓓ the Southern Hemisphere also has summer.

4. Why does the moon go through phases?

   Ⓐ Different parts of its lit half can be seen from Earth.

   Ⓑ It changes shape as it orbits Earth.

   Ⓒ Only small parts of the moon give off light at any one time.

   Ⓓ Light from the sun cannot always reach the moon.

5. Where is the moon located when people on Earth see a full moon?

   Ⓐ between Earth and the sun

   Ⓑ on the side of Earth opposite the sun

   Ⓒ on the side of the sun opposite to Earth

   Ⓓ in the same place as Earth

6. Why does a person on Earth see different constellations throughout the year?

(A) Stars move from one constellation to another.

(B) Constellations move across the sky.

(C) Earth travels to different points in its orbit.

(D) People are not good about making notes about constellations.

7. All planets rotate and revolve at different speeds. What units of time are determined by the length of rotation and revolution?

_____

_____

_____

8. Why are the seasons in the Northern Hemisphere opposite to those in the Southern Hemisphere?

_____

_____

_____

9. How did people use constellations to decide when to plant crops?

_____

_____

_____

Lesson 9

Naming Constellations

By quickly lifting the point of your pencil up and down, make a group of dots in the space below. When you are finished, connect some of the dots to form a picture. Find more than one picture if you can. Write a name for each picture. This is similar to how people named the constellations.

Lesson 9, Naming Constellations
Science 4, SV 9781419034329

Lesson 9   Constellation Stories

Read the following passage. Then answer the questions that follow the passage.

People have told stories and written about constellations for many, many years. Some of the stories are quite grand and have been passed down for centuries. Many come out of ancient Greek myths.

One such story is about a group of constellations, one of which is known as Andromeda. Andromeda was the daughter of a beautiful queen named Cassiopeia and a king named Cepheus. Cassiopeia used to brag about how beautiful she and her daughter were. One day she even said that they were more beautiful than the sea nymphs. This caused the king of the sea, Poseidon, to become very angry. He sent a sea monster to destroy the city in which Andromeda lived.

The story goes on to tell that the king found out about the monster. He went to a wise man known as an oracle to find out what to do. The oracle told him that Poseidon would call back the monster if he gave up his daughter. So the king brought his daughter to a tiny island and left her there. She would surely have died if it were not for a hero named Perseus.

Perseus was on his way home from winning a battle with another monster when he saw Andromeda. He rescued her, and both Andromeda and the city were saved. Constellations have been named for the characters from the story, including Andromeda, Cassiopeia, Cepheus, Perseus, and even the sea monster.

1. According to the story, why did Poseidon become angry?

   Ⓐ People of the town threw trash into the sea.

   Ⓑ Perseus came and took Andromeda away.

   Ⓒ Cassiopeia said that she was more beautiful than the sea nymphs.

   Ⓓ A monster had come to scare the nymphs of the sea.

2. What did the king decide to do when he found out about the monster?

   Ⓐ give up his daughter

   Ⓑ move to another city

   Ⓒ fight Poseidon

   Ⓓ call Perseus

3. What was Perseus's role in the story?

   Ⓐ He turned a group of stars into a girl named Andromeda.

   Ⓑ He made a constellation to look like Andromeda.

   Ⓒ He battled with Poseidon.

   Ⓓ He rescued Andromeda.

Lesson 9   Experiment: Investigating Moon Phases

Many stories are told about the moon. Early calendars were based on the moon. In this activity, you will make a model to learn why the moon goes through its phases.

What You Will Need

large ball
small ball
flashlight
one or two helpers

Procedure

1. Have a helper hold the large ball that represents Earth.
2. Have another helper shine the flashlight on the ball. Or place the flashlight on a desk so that it shines on the ball.
3. Hold the smaller ball near the large ball to represent the moon.
4. Dim the lights and move the smaller ball around the larger ball. At each position, draw how the moon looks to a person on Earth.

Analysis

D

C

A
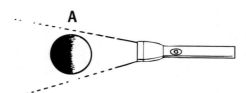

B

Experiment: Investigating Moon Phases (cont'd.)

1. At which point was a person on Earth able to see all of the lit half of the moon?

_____

_____

2. At which point was a person on Earth not able to see any of the lit side of the moon?

_____

_____

_____

Conclusion

Why does the moon go through a cycle of phases?

_____

_____

_____

Science Fair Projects

A science fair project is a way to find an answer to a question about the world. This type of project is a lot like the experiments you do as you study science. You follow many of the same steps.

The difference is that a science fair project takes a bit longer. It involves more time, research, and work. All science fair projects have many things in common.

Choose a Topic

The first thing you need to do is find a topic you like. Do you like animals, plants, or rocks? Maybe you prefer space, weather, or electricity. Decide on a topic you would like to learn about.

The next step is to ask a question about your topic. If you like rocks, you might ask,

"How is one rock different from another?"

If you like weather, you might ask,

"Can you predict the weather from the clouds you see?"

Gather Information

The next thing you need to do is to learn about your topic. You can use books, magazines, and the Internet.

You can also talk to people who might know about the topic. Maybe your project is about weather. You might ask a person who studies weather at a local news station.

Perhaps your project is about plants. You might speak with a gardener at a nearby nursery.

Types of Projects

There are three basic types of projects. What you need to do depends on the type you choose.

An Experiment An experiment is a series of steps you follow to answer your question. This type of project involves choosing a variable. The *variable* is something that you will change to find out what happens.

Suppose you grow two plants. They are the same in every way except for one. You add plant food to the soil of one plant. You do not add it to the other. Plant food is the thing you change. It is your variable.

You use your variable to state a hypothesis. A *hypothesis* is your guess about what you think will happen.

Your hypothesis might be that a plant that gets food will grow better. You don't know that this is true. You guess that it will be true. You will find out if you are right as you do your project.

To test your hypothesis, you design and conduct an experiment. Your *procedure* is the steps you follow. For example, you record how much plant food you add to one plant and when you add it. You record what else you do to the plants and where you put them.

You should make observations during the experiment. An *observation* is something you learn using your senses. You might make notes about how each plant looks. You might measure the height of each plant over time. You might make drawings of the plants or take photographs of them on different days. Any information you get is known as your *data*.

When you are finished, you *analyze your results*. This means that you think about your data. You try to figure out what the information means. For example,

you need to figure out if the plant with food grew better than the other plant.

You *draw a conclusion* by deciding what happened. You might conclude that the plant with food did grow better than the other plant.

At the end, you go back to the hypothesis. You must decide if your conclusion supports your hypothesis. In this case, it does. You thought that the plant food would help a plant to grow better and it did.

Keep in mind that your project is not a failure if your conclusion does not support your hypothesis. Your goal was to answer a question. Even if your conclusion tells you that the hypothesis was not true, you still learn something about your topic. The goal of science is to learn about the natural world.

An Exhibit Not all science projects involve experiments. Some science projects are used to teach other people about a topic.

This type of project can be a model, display, or demonstration. It should include an essay that describes the exhibit. It should have pictures that relate to the exhibit.

You can use this type of project to show a process. You might show what happens when a volcano erupts.

A Collection This type of project involves classifying objects. To *classify* means to place objects into groups by how they are alike and different.

For this type of project, you might

Science Fair Projects
Science 4, SV 9781419034329

gather a number of objects. The objects should be items from the natural world, such as rocks or leaves. They should not be objects that people make, such as stamps, coins, or toys.

You then study the objects and decide how to classify them. For example, you might group rocks by their color or sparkle. You might group leaves by their shape and size.

Once you put the objects into groups, you should write a name or description of each object. Your project must explain how you decided on your groups. It must also tell why you placed each object in a group.

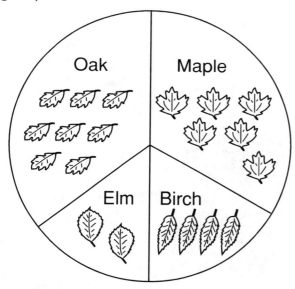

Safety

The most important part of any science fair project is to stay safe. Always listen to what your teacher or parent tells you.

Check with your teacher or parent before starting any project. If you are not sure if a material is safe, ask your teacher or parent. Let your teacher or parent know right away if anything breaks or spills.

Always wear safety goggles. These will protect your eyes from chemicals. They will also protect you from any materials that come loose.

If any substances do touch your eyes or skin, tell your teacher or parent right away. Flush your eyes or skin with running water for several minutes.

Tie back long hair. Don't wear loose clothing. Never taste, touch, or smell anything unless your teacher or parent tells you to.

Do not eat or drink around your project. Things from your project can get into your food. Your food might also ruin your project.

Project Notebook

Write down everything about your project. Keep your notes in a notebook that you can show to others. You should include the following information.

Title Page This page should list the title of your project. It should also include your name, your teacher's name, and the date.

Table of Contents This page should list everything in your report. It should

Science Fair Projects
Science 4, SV 9781419034329

also give the page number of each part of the report.

Overview This page should describe the purpose of the project. It should give a short description of what you did and what you learned.

If your project is an experiment, this page should present your hypothesis.

Materials This page should give a list of any materials you used. Tell the sizes of items or how many you used.

Experiment and Data Write all of the steps that you followed. Include drawings or photos of steps when possible.

Write notes about what you did and observed. Show graphs and charts of what you found.

Conclusion This page tells what you discovered during the project. It should also tell if your results supported your hypothesis.

Sources Anything you used to learn about your topic is called a source. List any written sources you used. Tell the name of the source. Tell who wrote or published the source and when.

List any people who gave you information. Give their titles and where they work.

Presenting the Project

Just as scientists share their results, you must show what you learned. You should show your science notebook.

You should also make a display. The display should be neat and easy to follow.

Your display should tell everything about your project. It should show any pictures, graphs, or charts you made. It should show any objects you collected. An example of how to display your project is shown below.

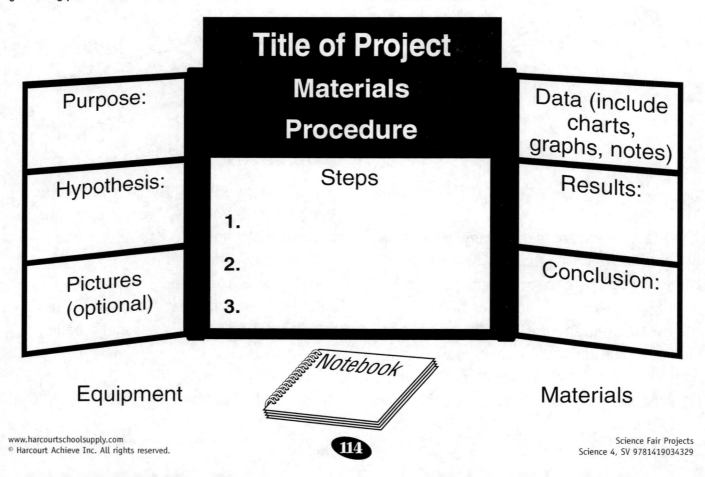

Project Ideas

There are many great ideas you can use for a science fair project. Here is a list of some questions that you might think about.

You might use one of them, or they might give you an idea for something completely different.

- **How does temperature affect the size of a gas?** Measure the size of a balloon that has been in sunlight, at room temperature, and in the freezer.

- **How can a substance change state?** Study the process through which solid ice turns to liquid water and then into water vapor.

- **Do soap bubbles last longer on warm or cold days?** Find out how long bubbles last at different temperatures.

- **How does the surface affect the speed of an object?** Compare the motion of a toy car on different surfaces, such as wood floor, carpet, and sandpaper.

- **How can you increase the speed of a wooden car?** Make a car and show how you can make the car go faster down a ramp. Consider changing the height of the ramp, the way the wheels are attached, and the surface of the ramp.

- **Do feathers and quarters fall at the same rate?** Drop objects from the same height and determine which one lands first. Find out how the shape of an object affects how fast it falls.

- **What materials are best at preventing heat from leaving an object?** Place a warm liquid in a container. Wrap the container in different materials, such as foil or paper. Find out which material lets the liquid cool off the fastest.

- **How does light reflect off different materials?** Shine light on different surfaces. Find out what happens to light as it hits each one. Change the direction from which you shine the light to see if it causes any change.

- **Do ants prefer certain kinds of food?** Find out if ants are attracted by specific foods.

- **Do mealworms travel faster on different surfaces?** Measure how far a mealworm moves on a surface in a specific amount of time. Compare the distance on different surfaces.

- **How long does it take for the heart rate to return to normal after exercise?** Compare the heart rate of a person before and after exercise. Find out what factors affect how fast the person's heart beats.

- **Does the distance to a light source affect how fast plants make food?** Place a water plant in a tank. Move a light source and use the bubbles made by the plant to compare how fast the plant makes food.

- **How does a caterpillar grow into a butterfly?** Follow the stages in the life cycle of a butterfly.

- **How do worms affect the soil?** Show how worms move through soil.

- **What are the layers of Earth?** Make a model showing inside Earth. Tell about the layers and how they affect the entire planet.

- **How does the pH of the soil affect plant growth?** Use a pH meter to measure the pH of samples of soil. Show how plants in the soil are affected by the soil's pH.

- **How do plants affect the rate of soil erosion?** Compare how soil washes away on a mound of uncovered soil and a mound of soil covered by plants.

- **Why don't other planets have liquid water?** Consider how the position of a planet affects its temperature. Show how the distance to the sun makes other planets too warm or too cold for liquid water. Investigate how the atmosphere of a planet affects its temperature as well.

- **How can you tell how far away a star is?** Show how you can use parallax to estimate the distance to a star.

- **Why are days and years shorter or longer on other planets?** Find out what determines the length of a day and year. Show how it is different on other planets.

- **How can a sundial tell time?** Build a simple sundial and use it to tell time.

GLOSSARY

asteroid—a small rocky object in space (p. 92)

axis—an imaginary line that runs from the North Pole to the South Pole of Earth (p. 101)

cell—the basic unit of living things (p. 44)

cellular respiration—the process through which an organism uses oxygen to release energy stored in food (p. 44)

charge—a positive or negative characteristic of a particle that exerts an electric force on other charged particles (p. 30)

chemical property—a characteristic of matter that can be observed only by changing the nature of the matter (p. 7)

circuit—a path through which electric current can flow (p. 30)

cleavage—a property of minerals that split along flat surfaces (p. 80)

comet—a small mass of ice and dust that orbits the sun in a long path (p. 92)

community—all of the populations of organisms living in the same place (p. 69)

conduction—the transfer of heat between particles of matter that are touching each other (p. 30)

constellation—a group of stars that has been given a name according to an imaginary picture it forms (p. 101)

consumer—an organism that must eat other living things to get energy (p. 69)

convection—the transfer of heat by currents formed in liquids and gases (p. 30)

cycle—a series of events that occurs over and over again (p. 57)

decomposer—an organism that breaks down wastes or bodies of dead organisms (p. 69)

density—the mass of an object divided by its volume (p. 7)

deposition—the process through which sediments are dropped in one place (p. 80)

distance—the length an object moves from a starting position (p. 19)

ecosystem—the living and nonliving things in an environment (p. 69)

electric current—the flow of electric charge (p. 30)

electric field—the push or pull that surrounds a charged particle (p. 30)

electromagnet—a wire carrying electric current that is twisted into loops and wrapped around an iron core (p. 30)

Glossary, cont'd.

energy—the ability to cause change (p. 30)

energy pyramid—a diagram that shows that the amount of available energy decreases along a food chain (p. 69)

erosion—the process through which natural forces, such as wind and water, carry away bits of rock and other materials over time (p. 80)

food chain—the flow of energy from producers to consumers in an ecosystem (p. 69)

food web—the overlapping food chains in an ecosystem (p. 69)

force—a push or a pull (p. 30)

fracture—a property of minerals that break apart unevenly (p. 80)

gas—the state of matter that has no definite shape and takes up no definite amount of space (p. 7)

generator—a device that uses a changing magnetic field to produce electric current (p. 30)

germinate—to sprout, as a plant seedling (p. 57)

heat—the transfer of thermal energy from a warmer object to a cooler one (p. 30)

igneous rock—a type of rock formed from the cooling of lava or magma (p. 80)

life cycle—the changes that occur to an organism between birth and death (p. 57)

liquid—the state of matter that takes up a definite amount of space but takes the shape of its container (p. 7)

magnet—an object that attracts materials, such as metals, to it (p. 30)

magnetic pole—a region of a magnet where the magnetic effects are strongest (p. 30)

mass—the amount of matter in an object (p. 7)

matter—any material or object that has mass and takes up space (p. 7)

metamorphic rock—a type of rock formed when high heat and pressure change one form of rock into another (p. 80)

metamorphosis—changes in the body and behavior of an organism (p. 57)

meteor—a piece of rock or dust that glows when entering Earth's atmosphere (p. 92)

meteorite—the remains of a meteor that reaches Earth's surface (p. 92)

meteoroid—a piece of rock or dust before it enters Earth's atmosphere (p. 92)

mineral—a solid, naturally occurring, inorganic crystal structure that has a definite chemical makeup (p. 80)

Glossary, cont'd.

motion—any change in the position of an object (p. 19)

opaque—not allowing light to pass through (p. 30)

orbit—the path an object follows as it travels around another object in space (p. 92)

organ—a group of tissues that work together to perform a task (p. 44)

organ system—a group of organs that work together to perform a task (p. 44)

organelle—a part of a cell that performs a task the cell needs to survive (p. 44)

organism—a living thing (p. 44)

phases of the moon—the changes in the appearance of the moon because of its motion around Earth (p. 101)

photosynthesis—the process through which an organism uses light energy to change carbon dioxide and water into food and oxygen (p. 44)

physical property—a characteristic of matter that can be observed without changing the nature of the matter (p. 7)

planet—a large object that moves around a star (p. 92)

population—all of the organisms of the same species living in one area (p. 69)

position—the location of an object (p. 19)

producer—an organism that can make food (p. 69)

radiation—the transfer of heat without the use of matter (p. 30)

reference point—a place or object used to describe the position or relative motion of an object (p. 19)

reflection—the bouncing of light off an object (p. 30)

refraction—the bending of light as it passes from one material to another at a slant (p. 30)

relative motion—a change in the position of an object when compared to another object or location (p. 19)

reproduction—the process through which organisms make more organisms like themselves (p. 44)

revolution—the movement of Earth around the sun (p. 101)

rotation—the spinning on an axis (p. 101)

satellite—an object that orbits a larger object in space (p. 92)

sediment—a small piece of solid material that has been broken down by weathering (p. 80)

Glossary, cont'd.

sedimentary rock—a type of rock formed when layers of sediment become squeezed and glued together by natural processes (p. 80)

solar system—a group of objects in space that move around a star (p. 92)

solid—the state of matter that has a definite shape and takes up a definite amount of space (p. 7)

species—a group of similar organisms that can reproduce (p. 69)

speed—the distance an object moves divided by the time during which it moves (p. 19)

spore—a cell that can grow into a new plant (p. 57)

star—a glowing ball of gas (p. 92)

static electricity—charge that does not flow (p. 30)

streak—the color of the powder left behind when a mineral is rubbed across a tile surface (p. 80)

thermal energy—the total energy of the particles in a sample of matter (p. 30)

tissue—a group of cells that work together to perform a task (p. 44)

translucent—relating to an object that reflects some light, absorbs some light, and transmits some light (p. 30)

transparent—relating to an object that allows most of the light hitting it to pass through (p. 30)

volume—the amount of space an object or material takes up (p. 7)

weathering—the process through which natural forces, such as wind and water, break down rocks and other materials into small pieces (p. 80)

zygote—the single cell that begins the human life cycle (p. 57)

Answer Key

Assessment, pages 5–6
1. C	**2.** D	**3.** B	**4.** D
5. A	**6.** B	**7.** D	**8.** B
9. C	**10.** A	**11.** D	**12.** C
13. B	**14.** C	**15.** D	**16.** A
17. B	**18.** C		

Unit 1 Lesson 1
Review, p. 11

1. B **2.** C **3.** D
4. A **5.** B **6.** B

7. Matter in every state is made up of moving particles. However, in the solid state, the particles are held closely together and only move back and forth in place. In the liquid state, the particles stay close together, but they can slide past one another. Particles in the gas state move at high speeds in all directions.

8. A physical property is one that can be observed without changing the type of matter. Color, texture, mass, volume, and density are physical properties. A chemical property is one that involves a change in the matter. The abilities to burn and to rust are chemical properties.

Properties of Matter, p. 12
Across

4. density   **5.** liquid
7. gram   **8.** volume
9. physical

Down

1. chemical   **2.** mass
3. matter   **5.** liter
6. solid   **7.** gas

Solids, Liquids, and Gases, p. 13
1. gas   **2.** mass
3. volume   **4.** physical
5. matter   **6.** chemical
7. density   **8.** solid
9. liquid

States of Matter, p. 14
Top diagram: gas; air, oxygen
Center diagram: liquid; milk, juice
Bottom diagram: solid; comb, cup

Titanic, p. 16
1. C   **2.** B   **3.** A   **4.** D

Experiment: Mass, Volume, and Density, p. 18
Analysis

1. The volume of the bottle did not change. It always stayed the same size.

2. The mass of the bottle increased as quarters were added to it.

Conclusion

The density of the bottle increased because it went from floating to sinking.

Unit 1 Lesson 2
Review, pp. 22–23

1. B   **2.** A   **3.** D
4. C   **5.** A   **6.** C

7. Answers will vary but should describe the bed relative to three objects or locations. For example, the bed is next to the dresser, below the window, or down the hall from the family room.

Answer Key cont'd.

8. Answers will vary but should describe that they are moving relative to objects outside the airplane. These might include the ground, objects on the ground, or objects in space such as the sun. They are not moving relative to objects on the plane, such as the plane itself, the seat, and other passengers also sitting in their seats.

9. The object is moving 10 kilometers per second (10 km/s). In 20 seconds, it will move 200 kilometers (20 s $\times$ 10 km/s).

Position, p. 24
Although they are not being judged on artistic ability, check student diagrams for accuracy. Make sure the descriptions of position are correct.

Position and Motion, p. 25
1. reference point
2. speed
3. position
4. distance
5. relative motion

Message: motion

Breaking the Sound Barrier, pp. 26–27
1. D   2. C   3. B   4. A

Experiment: Investigating Motion, p. 29
Analysis
1. Adding books to the stack increases the steepness of the ramp.
2. Increasing the steepness of the ramp increases the speed of the car.

Conclusion
The greater the speed of an object, the greater the distance it travels in a given amount of time. You can increase the distance an object moves in a period of time by increasing its speed.

Unit 1 Lesson 3
Review, pp. 36–37
1. C   2. A   3. D
4. A   5. D   6. C
7. B
8. The counter is warmer than the snowball. Heat is transferred from the counter to the snowball. This causes the counter to become cooler and the snowball to become warmer. Eventually, the snowball will melt.
9. An electromagnet is formed when a wire that can carry electric current is wrapped into a coil. An iron core is inserted into the coil. An electromagnet is useful because it can be turned on and off. It is also useful because it can be made stronger by adding more coils to the wire.

Answer Key cont'd.

Describing Forms of Energy, p. 38

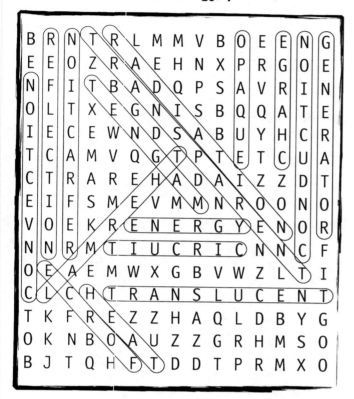

Heat Transfer, p. 39
1. radiation, heat from the sun
2. conduction, pot on a stove
3. convection, soup in a pot

Electric Circuits, p. 40
1. parallel circuit

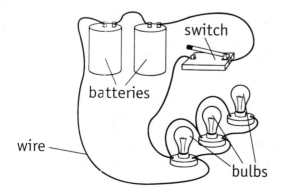

2. series circuit

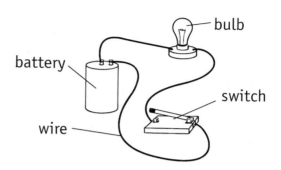

Comparing Forms of Energy, p. 41
1. energy
2. refraction
3. generator
4. Heat
5. force
6. reflection
7. circuit
8. charge
9. transparent
10. electromagnet

Experiment: Investigating Reflection, p. 43
Analysis

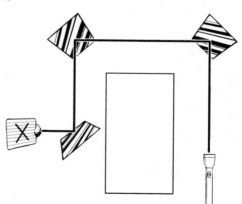

Conclusion
1. If you shine the light straight at a mirror, it bounces straight back from the mirror.

Answer Key
Science 4, SV 9781419034329

Answer Key cont'd.

2. I had to shine the light so it hit each mirror at a slant. This way, it bounced off at a slant and traveled to the next mirror.

Unit 2 Lesson 4
Review, pp. 49–50
1. A   2. D   3. B
4. C   5. B   6. A
7. Only plants conduct photosynthesis, but both plants and animals conduct cellular respiration. Only plants are able to capture sunlight to make food. However, both types of organisms need energy to survive, so both need to use cellular respiration to release stored energy.
8. The substances needed by cells must dissolve in water so they can be carried to cells and be used by them.

Types of Cells, p. 51
Plant and animal cells share most of the same organelles. However, only the plant cell has a cell wall, chloroplasts, and a large vacuole.

Prefixes, p. 52
1. Photosynthesis is the use of light to make food.
2. Reproduction is to make more organisms again.
3. She had to write it again.
4. He had to turn the tape back to the beginning.
5. She used light to make a picture of the class.

Describing Living Things, p. 53
1. cellular respiration
2. tissue
3. organelle
4. reproduction
5. photosynthesis
6. organism

Discovering Cells, p. 54
Hooke: Made up the name "cells"; Studied cork
Leeuwenhoek: Studied pond water; Saw living cells
Both: Used a microscope; Worked in the 1600s

Experiment: Getting Too Close, pp. 55–56
Analysis
1. to show that the seeds grow fine when they are alone
2. to show that each plant could grow in the same pot with another plant
Conclusion
They did not grow as well as they did in the other pots. The sweet potato plants must make something that prevents other plants from growing too close to them.

Unit 2 Lesson 5
Review, pp. 60–61
1. B   2. C   3. D
4. A   5. D   6. C
7. Incomplete metamorphosis does not have a larval stage. An egg hatches into a nymph. The nymph usually looks much like the adult. In complete

Answer Key cont'd.

metamorphosis, there are four distinct stages. The early stages look very different from the adult.

8. They both represent the first stage in the life cycle of an organism.

Growing Up, p. 62
Students should provide a descriptive paragraph about growing up.

Describing Change, p. 63
1. cycle
2. zygote
3. spores
4. metamorphosis
5. germinate

Insect Life Cycles, p. 64
The fly goes through complete metamorphosis because it has four stages. The early stages look very different from the adult stage.

The Monarch Butterfly, p. 66
1. C   2. B   3. A   4. D

Experiment: The Parts of a Flower, p. 68
Analysis
1. Some pollen sticks to the paper.
2. It had a stem, sepals, and seeds.
Conclusion
The fruit of the apple is the ovary. It protects the seeds inside.

Unit 2 Lesson 6
Review, p. 73
1. A   2. C   3. B
4. B   5. D   6. C
7. Animals cannot produce their own food. They eat plants or organisms that ate plants to get food. Food contains energy that animals need to survive.
8. Each organism uses some of the energy it obtains and stores the rest. In addition, some energy is changed into heat energy that is released into the environment. Only a small portion of the energy from each organism is passed on to the organism that eats it.

A Frozen Food Chain, p. 74
Diatom → Krill →
    Arctic Cod   → Seal → Polar Bear
        ↓   ↓
    Polar Bear   Arctic Wolf

Making Predictions, p. 75
1. bird and coyote
2. Mountain lions eat deer. The population of mountain lions will probably decrease because they will not be able to get enough food.
3. The deer, grasshopper, and prairie dog will be most directly affected because they feed on grass. All organisms will be indirectly affected because all of the organisms are interrelated.

Answer Key cont'd.

Describing Organisms, p. 76

Hidden Message: Organisms interact in an ecosystem.

Biomes of the World, p. 78
1. C **2.** D **3.** A **4.** B

Experiment: Insect Habitats, p. 79
Analysis
Answers will vary. Students should describe the insects. If they don't know their names, they should describe what they look like. If time allows, help students research the insects. Warn students to avoid touching insects.

Conclusion
If the places are far enough apart or in different conditions, students should find different insects. A place near a pond, for example, would have different insects than a place near a flowerbed.

Unit 3 Lesson 7
Review, pp. 84–85
1. C **2.** B **3.** D
4. C **5.** D **6.** A
7. It does not occur naturally.
8. The rock might be broken down by erosion. The resulting sediment might be piled up through deposition. Over time, pressure and chemical changes might change the sediments into solid rock.

Earth's Materials, p. 86
1. igneous
2. erosion
3. cleavage
4. minerals
5. Sedimentary
6. metamorphic
7. deposition
8. streak

Properties of Minerals and Rocks, p. 87
Across
1. hardness
3. mineral
4. luster
7. igneous rock
8. deposition
9. fracture

Answer Key cont'd.

10. erosion
11. streak
Down
2. rock cycle
3. metamorphic rock
5. rock
6. magnetite

The Grand Canyon, p. 89
1. D   **2.** A   **3.** C   **4.** B

Experiment: Investigating Weathering, p. 91
Analysis
1. Everything had to be kept the same except for the type of sugar. In this way, any differences in time measurements would be because of the type of sugar.
2. The granulated sugar has a greater surface area than the sugar cube because it is broken into small pieces of sugar instead of one solid piece.
3. The granulated sugar dissolved first.
Conclusion
The sugar broken into smaller pieces dissolved faster. In a similar way, a rock broken into smaller rocks will weather more quickly.

Unit 3 Lesson 8
Review, p. 96
1. A   **2.** C   **3.** D
4. B   **5.** C   **6.** D
7. The moon orbits a planet instead of the sun.

8. How often a comet is seen depends on its orbit. Some comets have very long orbits. It may take thousands of years for them to come close to the sun again. Others have shorter orbits. They may pass close to the sun more than once during a person's lifetime.
9. The sun was formed from gas and dust billions of years ago. Billions of years from now, the sun will run out of fuel. It will turn into a red giant. The outer layers of the sun will escape into space. A white dwarf will be left behind. In time, the white dwarf will fade out.

Shooting Stars, p. 97
1. Top object in space: meteoroid. A meteoroid is a piece of rock or dust before it enters Earth's atmosphere.
2. Object in sky: meteor. A meteor is a piece of rock or dust that glows as it enters Earth's atmosphere.
3. Object on ground: meteorite. A meteorite is the remains of a meteor that has reached Earth's surface.
All three are pieces of rock or dust. They differ in their location, either outside Earth's atmosphere, in Earth's atmosphere, or on Earth's surface.

Describing Objects in the Sky, p. 98
1. orbit   **2.** satellite
3. asteroid   **4.** planet
5. comet   **6.** meteor
7. star   **8.** solar system

Answer Key cont'd.

Supernovas, p. 99

1. It takes time for the light from the explosion to travel such long distances.
2. SN 2010D
3. Astronomers can calculate the distance to the star that exploded. If they know the galaxy the star is in, they can compare the distance with an earlier estimate. If the distance has increased, the astronomers can conclude that the galaxy has moved farther away. This means that the universe is getting larger.

Experiment: Investigating Star Brightness, p. 100

Analysis

1. The closer flashlight looked brighter each time.
2. I could move the brighter flashlight farther away than the other one.

Conclusion

The star must be at a greater distance away from Earth than the sun is.

Unit 3 Lesson 9

Review, pp. 105–106

1. C   2. D   3. B
4. A   5. B   6. C
7. One day is determined by the length of rotation. One year is determined by the length of revolution.
8. Except for the first day of fall and spring, one hemisphere points toward the sun and the other points away from it. This is because Earth's axis is tilted.

9. People can see different constellations during different times of the year. This is because of Earth's revolution. The constellations, then, change like the seasons. If a person knows that he or she always sees a certain constellation in the spring, that person will know it is time to plant crops.

Naming Constellations, p. 107

Students should find random pictures in their dots. Allow them to use their imaginations. Encourage students to make up stories to go with their pictures.

If time allows, let students repeat the activity by poking holes in black paper or aluminum foil. They can then place a small light behind the paper in a dark room. This will help them to see the "stars" they made.

Constellation Stories, p. 108

1. C   2. A   3. D

Experiment: Investigating Moon Phases, p. 110

Analysis

1. C   2. A

Conclusion

As the moon orbits Earth, the half of the moon facing the sun is always lit up. A person on Earth can see different parts of the lit half as it moves.

Answer Key
Science 4, SV 9781419034329